warp

M P Publishing Limited
12 Strathallan Crescent
Douglas
Isle of Man
IM2 4NR
British Isles

First Published by M P Publishing Limited 2010.

ISBN 978-1-84982-022-6
WARP

© Richard Falk, 2010.

Richard Falk asserts his moral right to be identified as the
author of this work.

Book and Cover Design by Maria Smith.

Printed by CPI Cox & Wyman, Reading, RG1 8EX

warp

by Richard Falk

*This book is dedicated to the lower and upper
sixth forms at Roedean and Benenden
(especially the tall, slender ones with porcelain
white skin and flaming long red hair).
So long as I've got a face
you'll never be short of somewhere to sit.*

TABLE OF CONTENTS

Part One: Jack.

———

Part Two: Fuck.

Hommage à Thomas Hardy
(only nowhere near as bloody boring): 7
The Lack of Little Grey Cells: 11
101 Uses For A Dead Trainspotter: 15
Fluffy Pink Fucks 'R' Us: 17
Come And See My Psychic Etchings: 23
Shagging (it helps to sell books): 27
A Cadaverous Lasagne: 31
Henry Gets A Surprise: 39
Invasion!: 41

———

Part Three: Spank.

A Load Of Bollards: 47
Blue Tit Blues: 59
Saggy Aggie In The Soaraway Sun: 63
Schoolgirls Ahoy!: 67

———

Part Four: Jugs.

Muffy And His Furry Friends
In The Land Of Muff: 73
Guernica Meets Farthing Wood: 85
C/U Fanny: 99

Part Five: God.

Virgins Off The Starboard Bow: 111
Three-Headed Dog: 121
Beef Curtains With Tea: 133
Demons At Dawn: 137
Sorry, Can't Think Of A Witty Title
For This One: 147
Jack (Again): 149
Full Circle: 151

Epilogue.

Appendices.

Part One: Jack.

It was the kind of night that chilled the stoutest of hearts and set already weakened nerves on edge.

A low, greenish mist clung to the Thames, rising stealthily to envelop the city in a sinister phosphorescent glow. Shop girls hurried home to their lodgings, hearts pounding, and bolted and shuttered their doors behind them, lest their stiff corpses be found in the morning, their features set into a ghastly death rictus. Once inside, they would very quickly pray that their souls might reach the dawn alive.

For throughout the autumn of 1888, a pall of fear had gripped Whitechapel, like the impenetrable murk that now seized its gloomy, cobbled streets. Terrible rumours abounded of a maniac, a disfigured, murderous maniac who savagely slaughtered innocent young girls and left their mutilated bodies as grisly trophies for the sickened Peelers to find.

Yet one figure cut purposefully through the mist, and showed no signs of fear. It was a tall, gaunt man clad elegantly in a swirling black opera cape, which surmounted a hand-tailored dark suit of the finest quality. His thin, mean lips, offset by a pencil-thin moustache, framed a grim and humourless smile. In one of his piercing, coal-black eyes, a monocle glinted; a glossy top hat sat in uneasy repose atop his head.

As he took each measured, near-silent step, he encountered no other human life; until suddenly, a street urchin, dressed in grimy rags, stepped inadvertently into his path. The boy was transfixed in terror, petrified by the gleaming monocle, and caught in the man's evil, whistling breath. Then the sinister figure cried "Begone, boy!", and the lad scuttled back into the mist, offering silent thanks to Jesu that he had escaped with his throat uncut.

The sinister walker resumed his precise, purposeful steps. Out of the mist clattered a hansom cab, its driver braced against the cold and damp. The man flagged down the cab, barked an instruction to the driver, and flopped into the padded upholstery as though exhausted. The driver glanced surreptitiously at the reflection of his eerie client in the mirror, and shuddered involuntarily. Then he whipped the horses, and the hansom hurtled off into the night, and was swallowed up by the fog.

That night, in old London town, there were no fewer than nought savage murders, leaving us to commence our tale on a sunny Tuesday morning in Hemel Hempstead in April 1972.

Part Two: Fuck.

Chapter One
Hommage à Thomas Hardy
(only nowhere near as bloody boring).

Dartmoor is even further away from Hemel Hempstead, but at least we have reached the year 1972. As anyone who has visited it *(which I haven't)* can testify, Dartmoor is a supremely desolate and poetic place.

Craggy peaks and sparse valleys undulate like the scaly back of some prehistoric monster, whilst small animals chitter and forage for the tiniest scraps of food and comfort. A milky-white sun burns faintly in a harsh blue-grey sky yet fails to impart warmth to the eerie landscape.

A breath of wind stirs, and the reedy grasses bend unwillingly, as though forced by a giant – *but no, that's enough of that sort of crap. If you want Thomas Hardy, you'll find him under "H". Or possibly "T", if you're shopping at WH Smith.*

Anyway, Dartmoor's remote location makes it the ideal place for a high security prison, and in 1972 Dartmoor jail was under the control of one Willie Dykes, a man of extraordinarily lateral thinking, especially after a bottle or two of his favourite scotch.

Whereas other prison governors simply concentrated on preventing their inmates from escaping,

Mr. Dykes was always on the lookout for profit-making opportunities. One such possibility was presented by the prison canteen, which, naturally enough, was closed for business from six each night until eight the following morning. Consequently, the thought occurred that it might be the perfect venue for pre-Christmas corporate parties and sales presentations.

Shortly afterwards, a series of supremely tasteless advertisements began appearing in the marketing trade press. These featured the headline "Enjoy a captive audience this Christmas", with a picture of a man in a suit wearing a ball and chain – the ball, naturally enough, being an enormous plum pudding.

The genesis of the campaign was not without its problems. Dykes had gone right to the top and engaged London's most fashionable creative hotshop, Rosenkratz & Rosenkratz.

Unfortunately, this being 1972, there were still plenty of unreconstructed hippies around, who refused to work on the campaign on the basis that many of the prison's inhabitants were there only for their beliefs. Surprisingly, Dykes was only too happy to concur, citing the case of a prisoner who was serving a 10-year stretch for his belief that robbing banks with a fake sawn-off shotgun was a good way to get rich quickly.

When his exhortations of "This could be an award-winner, already!" and "My life, we're going to lose the account!" had failed, creative director Israel Rosenkratz was forced to resort to freelance talent to complete his campaign. His principal copywriter was one David Camp, of 23 Ophelia Drive, Hemel Hempstead.

Just around the corner from Mr. Camp lived one John Harrison, who is the real hero of our story, although strangely Harrison had never met David Camp or even spoken to him.

John Harrison was a very mild-mannered businessman, who, just like Reginald Perrin in *The Fall And Rise Of Reginald Perrin*, always walked down a series of roads named after poets to get to the railway station, and always caught the same train, which usually arrived about 11 minutes late. Unlike Reggie Perrin, however, he did not have an affair with his secretary, did not imagine his mother-in-law as a hippopotamus *(although if you had ever met Mrs. Ethel Beelzebub, you could have understood it if he had)*, did not fake his own suicide, and did not start up a chain of shops selling utter rubbish.

Indeed, he never did anything much apart from carrying out his job as a certified accountant at Pratt, Pratt & Pratt with extreme diligence and enthusiasm. Until one morning in April 1972, when he had a big shock on his way to the office: he discovered a bleeding corpse lying in the gutter.

"It's a bleeding corpse!" he exclaimed, and was promptly admonished for his bad language by a passing Salvation Army bigwig, on his way to buy a new Lamborghini with the proceeds of a tea and biscuit morning that had accidentally found their way into the inside pocket of his uniform.

After a few minutes, the police arrived breathlessly in the shape *(and a bloody odd one it is too)* of Detective Sergeant Harry Hogg. The preliminary "Evenin' all"s *(rather inappropriate, since it was 8.30 in the morning)* and "What's going on 'ere then?"s having been dispensed with, Hogg took a perfunctory look at the body.

"Well, he's dead," he concluded thoughtfully. "And I'd say he's been stabbed."

And indeed, it seemed the wily policeman was correct on both counts, as the pool of blood around the man's body and the knife sticking out of his ribs proved.

"Better get him collected," said Hogg, reaching for his radio. "And then I'll set about catching his killer."

(In case you're wondering what happened to John Harrison, I have no idea. Rosenkratz & Rosenkratz went on to become the world's largest advertising agency, before disgracing itself in an abortive attempt to buy a top five building society. Willie Dykes was dismissed following an incident of gross indecency with a warder and a vanilla blancmange, and as for David Camp: yes, he did live up to his name.)

Chapter Two
The Lack of Little Grey Cells.

At times like these, Hogg usually called in a little outside help from his friend, the "celebrated" detective Henri LaFarge. Monsieur LaFarge *(or Henry Roberts to his mother)* modelled himself on Agatha Christie's Hercule Poirot, and indeed there were many similarities between the two men, except that Henri LaFarge is not Belgian, does not have a silly moustache, does not live in a posh London mansion flat, and is not a very good detective.

Oh, all right then: they have nothing at all in common, but Henry is a thoroughly nice chap, and you can't blame him for trying.

Back at the station, Hogg picked up the phone and ordered a large deep pan pepperoni pizza. His stomach rumbling with anticipation, he then called LaFarge's number, and demanded his immediate presence at the police station.

"*Mais oui, mon ami,*" responded LaFarge, momentarily forgetting that his friend knew he was about as Belgian as a Yorkshire pudding. "*Immédiatement.*"

And with that, he switched on the answering machine *("Allo, mon ami, this is Henri LaFarge, private investigateur…"),* waved a greeting to

Mr. Entrails the butcher, from whom he rented the upstairs room, and slowly sprinted the few hundred yards to the police station.

Back at the station, Hogg put down the phone with satisfaction, and then sat back to mull over the facts of the case. He was sure he had done everything by the book, and yet there was an uneasy, niggling feeling that he had made some terrible mistake or omission that could have serious consequences.

For the next five minutes he wracked his brain, until the answer finally came to him. Of course: he had failed to specify *double* pepperoni.

As Hogg lamented the consequences of his error, LaFarge arrived imperiously in the station's reception.

"Henri LaFarge to see DS Hogg," he said to the WPC on reception.

"DS Hogg says he's busy interviewing, but he's lying," said the girl, and promptly showed Henry through.

In his office, Hogg was devouring the last of a Marks and Spencer cheese and onion quiche, huge gobbets of the filling clinging to his unruly beard.

"Hogg!" cried LaFarge, delighted to see his old friend.

"I resent that allegation," Hogg spluttered indistinctly, through a mouthful of quiche. "I've hardly eaten a thing all day. But sit down, my old pal, sit down."

"So, *mon ami*, what's all this about?" said Henry.

"Murder," said Hogg bluntly. "Very unpleasant

one. Shall we go and see the body? Better be quick,
I've a pizza that should be here in half an hour."

Chapter Three
101 Uses For A Dead Trainspotter.

The police mortuary was so cold it made Henry shiver. The place always reminded him of a supermarket cold store, and the whitened corpse, now bloodless and neatly wrapped in cellophane, strongly reminded him of a Sainsbury's frozen chicken. Except that the body bag did not display the price, sell-by date, calorific value or weight of its contents.

"His name's Alan Evans," explained Hogg. "Aged thirty-one. Well known around these parts as a passionate trainspotter."

And indeed, among the small pile of the man's personal possessions was a dog-eared British Rail timetable, some of its pages mysteriously stuck together. By its side was a little pocket diary, which Henry began to read.

"Pretty nasty stabbing," said Hogg. "Knife was thrust about six inches into his chest cavity, which would require quite some strength. So on that basis I'd say we're looking for a man."

"And our friend Evans was clearly looking for a woman," said Henry. "He has a date with a young lady called Julie Johnson on Friday, at the Two-And-A-Half Stoats. His diary says she's blonde, 5'2", slimly built, and will be wearing a black skirt and red sweater. Odd that he should describe her, don't you think?"

Hogg shrugged. All was revealed when Henry discovered, tucked into the back of the diary, a business card from Melanie Peachblossom, Consultant Director with the Findafuck dating agency of Knightsbridge. "Aha!" cried Henry. "Looks like our old friend Evans hasn't been getting his oats!"

"I daresay he hasn't," replied Hogg sheepishly, who had met his own ample wife Doris through the Lovehunger Singles Club, a dating agency especially for very greedy people. "So what do you suggest we do next?"

"Well, I'll have to keep our friend Evans's date with the mysterious Miss Johnson. But first, I'll join the agency and see if I can find any of the other women he met. That might lead me to the killer."

"But… but…" spluttered Hogg. "It could be incredibly dangerous, old friend. They could be demented, depraved, sex-starved…"

"I know," smirked Henry. "That's a risk I'll just have to take."

Chapter Four
Fluffy Pink Fucks 'R' Us.

It was always with a sense of relief that Henry left the depressing surroundings of Hemel Hempstead behind. *(Note to Hemel Hempstead Tourist Board: there's no point in suing me. All my money is in my cat's name.)*

As the dirty, smelly train crawled towards London, Henry reviewed the facts of the case in his mind. Certainly, there was no shortage of people with a motive to kill Alan Evans: rail passengers outraged by his "whoo! whoo!"s as the slow train struggled out of Hemel Hempstead; women disgusted by his fumbling and amateurish advances; and manufacturers of anoraks, whose products were brought into disrepute by Evans and his trainspotting chums. Possibly the whole matter was trainspotting related: perhaps a dispute had broken out between rival gangs over who had first spotted the new class D1X2Z diesel locomotive with twin Wankel *(I didn't make this up, I swear)* engines.

Crunching the last of his British Rail coffee as the train limped into Euston, Henry donned his coat and headed purposefully for the bright lights of Knightsbridge.

When he arrived, he found that the offices of Findafuck International were, unsurprisingly, pink and fluffy. Very pink, in fact, and very fluffy. On his arrival, Henry was seated on a pink sofa by a fluffy blonde girl in pink, who gave him a weak cup of tea in a blue cup *(surprised you there, didn't I?)*, and told him that Melanie Peachblossom would be along shortly.

And indeed she was, an imposing blonde middle-aged lady, made up to look younger, and dressed in a skin-tight white suit with miniskirt.

"How *do* you do?" The accent was cut-glass, the proffered hand as soft as butter. "Won't you come through, Mr. LaFarge?"

They walked down a short corridor into a large, very cold room. "This is the computer room," said Melanie Peachblossom, "and that's the computer itself. We call it Cupid. Amazing to think the amount of joy that wonderful machine has brought into so many lives."

The computer was a large, box-like thing, about the size of an office desk. Reels of tape whirred fitfully as it processed names and addresses, and a mass of green-and-white-striped listing paper chugged out of an orifice and zig-zagged untidily across the floor. *(Yes, I know computers don't actually look anything like this, but this novel is set in 1972, remember? Wakey, wakey!)*

"Very impressive," said Henry, his nostrils twitching at the faint smell of burning that was coming from the overworked machine.

"Come into my office," said Peachblossom

seductively, "and I'll tell you more about the company." Henry did so, and took a seat – which was, unsurprisingly, both pink and fluffy. "Well, my partner Heather Dovecottage and I set up Findafuck in 1968. One just grew so sad at seeing all the lonely people, who only wanted someone to love. But Findafuck isn't a conventional computer dating agency: oh no!"

She made an expansive gesture.

"You see, I believe we are all children of the cosmos, and that fate rules our destiny. That's why we will only introduce you to people whom you were destined to meet anyway. You see, man has become removed from his true inner self. How today would a courtly knight meet his robed lady, would Romeo encounter his Juliet, would Valentino meet his… er… er… Mrs. Valentino? I see us as the matchmakers of modern days, which is of course why we only advertise in the finest publications, to win the most discerning clients."

"Like this one, you mean?" Henry picked up a porn mag that had been lying around on the office coffee table. This prominently featured a Findafuck advertisement with the headline "Tired of wanking? Got cramp?", and a picture of a naked young girl lying on her back with her legs spread.

"That was a mistake," snapped Melanie Peach-blossom, snatching *(no pun intended)* the magazine from him. "The person who placed that got fired." Suddenly she was all bunny-wunny sweetness and light again. "So sir, the time has come to find the lady of your destiny, your queen and consort, your Guinevere." She handed him an application form. "Our service is fully guaranteed," she added conspiratorially.

"Do you guarantee I will meet the partner of my celestial dreams?" enquired Henry, falling in with her courtly patterns of speech.

"Not quite," said Melanie Peachblossom, handing him a small scrap of paper. On it was printed the message: **Findafuck Guarantee: A really satisfying hand job within six months or half your money back**. Henry winced.

"I'll give you five minutes to fill in the form," said the imperious blonde, rising to leave. "Please make sure you do so fully, because only that way can we match you with your ideal partner."

Henry promised that he would, and duly completed every section of the form, which requested his name, address, telephone number, penis size and preference for women with large or small breasts. Presently Peachblossom returned, congratulated him on having been so thorough, and led him back to the computer room where the data was fed into the machine. The giant device whirred and coughed and spluttered, and the smell of burning became worse than ever. Peachblossom tore a scrap off the snake of listing paper, and sealed it an envelope, then relieved Henry of a hefty cheque. Additional names were available, she confirmed, at one pound fifty the half-dozen.

Back on the street, Henry had a sudden desire to rip open the envelope and view its contents immediately, but restrained himself until he was back on the train. When he did so, he was delighted to see that Julie Johnson topped the list. She would definitely be his first port of call. Two of the other names could be discounted immediately: Mr. Andrei Kartelopovich of Eastcheap was out on the grounds of sex, whilst Miss Heather MacGregor of 4 The Only Street, Kyle of Lochalsh, was probably too remote even for a sex-starved trainspotter. The other three names were all in and around the Hemel Hempstead area, and meant nothing to him. But first he would meet Julie Johnson in Alan Evans's place, and then he, Henri LaFarge, master detective, would bring Alan Evans's killer to justice.

(Author's note: This book is getting bloody exciting, isn't it? And there you were, thinking it was some old shit about murders in Victorian England. Of course, you may have bought it wanting a book about murders in Victorian England, in which case you have my commiserations – but no refund. Anyway, you'll be delighted to know that the chapter after next is extremely pornographic, but no flicking ahead, please.)

Chapter Five
Come And See My Psychic Etchings.

The Two-And-A-Half Stoats *(whose landlord strenuously denied that he was attempting to poach business from the nearby, and long-established, Three Ferrets)* was a large and rather unpleasant pub on the outskirts of the village *(sorry, Hemel Hempstead, town)*, that was demolished back in 1974 as part of a road-widening exercise. With fake real fires, plastic horse brasses aplenty and several strategically placed shaggy sheepdogs *(whose owners were bribed to attend with free pints)*, it was highly popular with the chic commuting crowd, who thought it extremely quaint and rural.

Henry was, therefore, forced to fight off several visions in Barbour jackets before he finally spotted Julie Johnson, sitting demurely at a wobbly table, nursing an orange juice. She was very young indeed, he thought, probably about twenty-three, slim and pretty. That dirty old sod Evans, he thought, must be nearly ten years her senior! Of course, that made him fourteen, fifteen… never mind, he consoled himself, a man is only as old as the woman he feels.

"Hello," he said nervously. "You must be Julie."

She smiled thinly. "And you must be Alan. But where's your anorak?"

"Sorry?"

"The dirty old anorak you said you always wear. Nearly put me off coming."

He sat down heavily. "I'm not Alan," he said shortly. "Alan's dead. I'm a private detective, investigating his murder."

Her eyebrows shot up. "Alan's been murdered?"

"Aha!" Henry cried. "How did you know that? I only said he was dead."

"Yes, and then you said you were investigating his murder."

Shit! That wasn't how Sherlock Holmes would have handled it! Obviously he hadn't quite got the hang of that ploy yet, so he might as well be nice to her.

"Could I get you a drink anyway?" he stammered.

Draining her orange juice, she replied, "Yes, a champagne cocktail, please."

Oh fuck! Did he have enough money? And was this an allowable professional expense? he wondered, as he ordered the drinks from Bert Snout, the grim-faced landlord.

Julie Johnson slurped her cocktail in an unlady-like manner, and then proceeded to tell Henry all about herself in minute detail. She was, it transpired, twenty-two, lived alone, did not get on with her parents, and was looking for a soul-mate for "fun, laughter and you-know-what" – and believed she was being pursued by tiny, invisible leprechaun-like creatures. Henry tried to remember his basic psychology training: did this make her a schizophrenic or a psychopath? Either way, it made her a most unreliable witness, and a far more likely suspect.

"They follow me all the time," she insisted. "My doctor says the tablets will keep them at bay, but I know they're just waiting for their moment, to strike."

"Yes, well…" Henry coughed. "Tell me what you know about Alan Evans."

"Not much. He rang me last Wednesday, and we arranged to meet tonight. Said he liked train-spotting, hadn't had a woman for years, and had met four girls so far through the agency. One of them he liked a lot and had seen a few times – Brenda, I think it was. Very eccentric, he said she was. You get some bloody nutters in this club," she added sharply, staring pointedly at our not-very-intrepid hero, who tried not to laugh.

"Tell you what," she continued, "would you like to come back to my flat and have a look at the drawing I've done of Barney? He's the chief gnome who organises all the others. I've never seen him, mind, but his psychic currents are incredibly strong."

"Oh, I don't know…" began Henry, rather worried lest he become the next victim of the strange woman and her bizarre paranoia.

"Or would you just prefer a fuck?" she mused, leaning forward and exposing her cleavage.

See, I told you this book would start to get exciting if you waited long enough.

Chapter Six
Shagging
(it helps to sell books).

Right, I've caught you. You didn't even read that last chapter, did you? You just skipped ahead to this one to read the smutty bit. Well, just for that I'm not going to have a sex scene after all. I've got my art to think about, so there.

No, no… don't put this back on the shelf. I'm only joking. You'll get your smut, because I need the money.

So, where were we? Oh yes, our mate Henry had accompanied the totally mad Julie back to her house to give her a damn good seeing-to. And so…

Julie Johnson poked her head cautiously around the door. "Cuthbert? Mungo?" she called, then after a pause, "Good, they're all out. We can have our fuck in peace."

With that, she closed the door behind her, and began to remove her blouse. Off came the lacy white bra, revealing pert young breasts with inviting, swollen, pinkish-brown nipples. Now breathing heavily, she slipped off her tight skirt, and then her lacy little knickers, through which Henry could see her mound of pubic hair. Finally, she was totally naked, and strode over to the trembling Henry, and began to undress him.

As soon as his shirt was off, she began licking and nuzzling at his nipples, as her hand reached down to knead his throbbing member through his trousers. At the same time, he reached up and began to caress her heaving breasts, feeling the nipples harden as he did so.

She plunged her young, eager, thrusting tongue into Henry's receptive mouth, as with her other hand she finally undid his trousers. Wrenching his underpants to the floor, she knelt down and took his throbbing cock into her mouth, and began to suck greedily.

(Author's note: Why do women in pornographic stories always suck blokes' cocks "greedily"? Do none of them get three square meals a day? And why does shagging always sound better in basic Anglo-Saxon: "throbbing cocks" rather than "undulating penises"? Don't know, but it does.)

Henry began to moan, as her expert tongue brought him close to orgasm, then he reached down, pulled her head from his penis, swung his body across hers and entered her tight little pussy. *(Yes, I know this is physically impossible if his trousers and underpants are still around his ankles, but give me a little bit of artistic licence, OK?)*

She began to writhe and groan as he thrust harder and harder into her lithe young body, each stroke of his throbbing prick bringing her to higher planes of ecstasy. Finally, they came together, his fluid gushing into the depths of her nubile quim as she shrieked with delight. Then they lay still, the quiet of the late evening broken only by their laboured, contented breathing.

Finally, Julie Johnson sat up for no apparent reason, and said, "Bugger. That sounds like the gnomes coming home, and they'll be wanting their supper. I think it's time for you to go."

Chapter Seven
A Cadaverous Lasagne.

I owe you an apology. That sex scene was pathetic. There was I, getting you all excited for page after page of hardcore adult filth, and… 336 words. That's all I could manage. I have ejaculated prematurely on my word processor. (Not literally, you understand: the cleaner would have a fit.)

Oh well, I shall just have to do what I do when these little disappointments happen in real life, and say "Never mind, we can try again in the morning, after I've made you a nice breakfast, and this time it'll last for hours". Of course, this line works better if you can actually cook, unlike me…

The following morning, Henry woke up early, slightly relieved to have escaped the odd girl's flat unscathed, and immediately checked his Findafuck list. Yes, there it was: Brenda Bloomfield of 27 Paddock Lane, Bletchley. Another possible killer of Alan Evans, and his next date. His next fuck, even, with a bit of luck. Already he was seriously considering maintaining his Findafuck membership even after the case was solved, and he had several mates who could benefit from the service too.

As luck would have it, Brenda Bloomfield was

in, and Henry was delighted to note that she had a deep, husky, sensuous voice. She was, it turned out, twenty-three, and worked for the social services. She was also free that night, and so Henry agreed to meet her at her house at half past six.

When he arrived, he was greeted by a remarkably statuesque blonde beauty. Brenda Bloomfield was about 6'1", and must have weighed at least fifteen stones, although most of it looked like firm, muscular flesh rather than fat. She had an elegant, slightly ironic face, thick sensual lips and cascades of long, pale blonde curls. More significantly, her huge, heaving breasts, straining at a tight pink-and-white top, were virtually at Henry's eye level. An erection began to swell in his trousers as he realised the evening's date might end the same way as the last.

"Hello, Henri," she said huskily. "You're a very big boy." Henry smiled wanly. "I would invite you in," she continued, "but my cat's just had diarrhoea all over the living room floor, and it stinks to high heaven. So I thought we'd go out for an Italian instead, if that's all right with you."

Henry nodded, and they wandered along to the restaurant, chatting as they went.

La Casa Mafiosi turned out to be a typical mid-market Italian trattoria, with a bright white, red and green frontage, and a number of tables outside. There was a chilly breeze, and so Henry and Brenda elected to sit indoors.

She was clearly a regular customer, as she

greeted Roberto, the slimy, over-effusive proprietor, by name. He responded with a sentence in Italian, which Henry did not fully understand, although he was aware that it was some kind of a sexual insult. Clearly, this was part of an ongoing game between patron and customer.

Brenda quickly ordered spaghetti carbonara, whilst Henry settled for lasagne verdi, and they flopped back in their wicker chairs to chat.

"So, you're a social worker, then?" said Henry, as the chianti arrived. He was struggling to take his eyes off Brenda's huge, heaving chest.

"That's what I always say to people," she replied, "but I lied. People don't tend to want to go out with me if they know what I really do."

Henry was intrigued. "And what's that?"

She looked him directly in the eye. "I'm a mortician's assistant," she said. "I handle stiffs."

Now she was definitely flirting. Henry felt a lump beginning to form in his trousers. At this moment, the sexual tension was broken by the arrival of their food.

"That's – er – very interesting," he said, as he shifted uncomfortably in his chair.

"It is," she replied, taking her first mouthful of food, "fascinating. The human corpse is of great interest to me. I also like the tools we use – the hacksaws, scalpels and gougers. My favourite is the nutcracker-like implement we use to open the skull. KER-RUNCH! It's an amazing sound, and then the brain starts to ooze out."

Henry's erection was rapidly subsiding, and he

was starting to feel distinctly queasy. He wished the strange woman would shut up about her ghastly profession, but she continued unabated.

"Of course, the worst time is the summer. They start to stink very quickly if you don't keep them chilled, particularly when you slice open the stomach and release all the gases. Last year we had one that had been kept in a flat for three weeks in August with the heating full on. It stank like hell. Bright green, it was – and writhing with maggots."

Henry gagged, and pushed his bubbling green lasagne away from him. "I seem to have lost my appetite."

"Never mind," said Brenda Bloomfield, shovelling huge mouthfuls of food into her capacious mouth. "Shall we go our separate ways after the meal, or would you like me to take you up The Back Passage?"

Sadly for Henry, this turned out not to be an invitation to a new sexual experience, but a request to go clubbing. The Back Passage lived up to its name, being located in a very dingy passageway just off Queen's Road, on the outskirts of Bletchley.

The doorman looked suspiciously at them as they went in, and Henry was immediately uncomfortable. Inside, The Back Passage seemed a pleasant enough place, but the clientele were decidedly odd. Half the women seemed to be at least six feet tall, with very long blonde hair and ridiculously revealing lycra dresses, whilst the other half had their hair cropped short and wore dungarees.

The majority of the men had spiky cropped hair and thick bushy moustaches, and wore tight jeans and lumberjack shirts. A few feet away from Henry, a bunch of young lads were chatting, clad only in tight black leather trousers. In one case, Henry concluded, the lad must have run out of money to buy his and settled for a factory reject, since there was a huge hole where the seat should have been, revealing his gleaming hairless buttocks. Never mind, Henry thought, the bloke could always put over a patch later.

Brenda was speaking into his ear, explaining that the place was owned by a psychopathic Hell's Angel known to his friends as "Sweetie", but Henry was more interested in a conversation taking place between two moustachioed gentlemen.

"So how was your holiday, then?" one was saying to the other.

"Oh, it was lovely, dear. I simply adore camping in the South of France."

"No, lovey," said his friend. "You wouldn't catch me doing that. I simply can't stand sleeping in tents."

"Tents?" said the other, bemused. "We weren't in tents. We had a very nice four-star hotel."

A sharp tug from Brenda brought Henry back to reality. "You're not listening," she said firmly. "I was saying, there's a stripper on later. Do you like strippers?"

"Oh yes," said Henry dreamily. His erection began to swell again as he fantasised about a young, slim, eighteen-year-old blonde slowly revealing her firm young body for all in the club to enjoy. "What's her name, then?"

"Big Ben."

Henry shuddered, as he finally put two and two together. "I've got a better idea. Why don't we go back to your place for a quick shag?"

"That's just what I intended," said Brenda seductively, "but first…"

And with that, she seized Henry in her powerful arms, and thrust her tongue deep into his mouth. Hardly able to breathe, but fully enjoying himself, Henry reached up and slipped his hand inside her top and bra, kneading her soft, pliant breasts. After a few minutes in their passionate embrace, they were interrupted by a firm tap on Henry's shoulder.

He turned round to see a large, angry-looking bouncer. "Oi," said the doorman. "What d'you think you're doing? This is a gay club, you know. Our punters don't want to see things like that."

Brenda whispered something into the bouncer's ear. "No you're not," he said firmly, "you're a bloody woman. And Sweetie's not here, so he can't vouch for you. He broke one of his nails on a beer pump, and went home crying. Now fuck off, the pair of you – we don't want your sort in here."

A very crestfallen Brenda shuffled out into the night air with Henry, who was not at all despondent. After all, their premature ejection *(or should that be ejaculation?)* meant that he was a couple of hours closer to his promised shag.

Chapter Eight
Henry Gets A Surprise.

On arrival back at the house, Brenda showed Henry into the sitting room, and warned him to be careful of the pool of cat's diarrhoea that covered most of the floor. As she went off to change, Henry walked gingerly around the room looking for clues, and trying very hard not to breathe in.

The stench of the cat's diarrhoea was absolutely indescribable: not like normal catshit at all, but a sweet, sickly, noxious aroma like nothing on earth. The lounge was almost devoid of personal items: there was no desk or chest for Henry to rummage through, and so he contented himself with examining a very odd fragment of a strange metal he had never seen before, displayed as an ornament on the mantelpiece.

As he picked it up, Brenda re-entered the room and said "Careful with that! Don't drop it whatever you do!", making Henry jump.

"Sorry," said Henry, putting the ornament back down. Brenda had changed into a long, flowing white nightdress with a low-cut, lacy top that clearly revealed her soft, swollen breasts. As Henry's trousers began to billow, she took him by the hand and led him into the bedroom.

Henry's erection swelled as she fiddled with his zip, and he reached up and slipped the straps of her nightdress from her shoulders. As she began to caress his throbbing member, he kneaded her pliant breasts, and groaned with ecstasy.

Getting bolder now, he reached downwards, in search of her moist, inviting, tight little pussy.

As his hand found its target, his scream could be heard throughout Paddock Lane.

Chapter Nine
Invasion!

Henry spent a night wracked with terrible nightmares, and woke up in a cold sweat. For a moment he thought the previous night's events had all been a grotesque dream, then realisation came back to him and he retched.

As he washed, he tried to get the evening's events into some kind of perspective. He could not even remember what had happened after he discovered "Brenda"'s terrible secret; how he had got home and when was a complete blur, subordinated in his mind to the unbelievable moment when he had discovered that "Brenda Bloomfield" was in fact an alien.

What other explanation could there be? The entity was definitely a woman, and yet equally definitely had a large and throbbing penis. No human woman had a willy, so there was no other possible explanation.

The strange metal object corroborated this conclusion. Clearly it was part of a spacecraft that the entity was concealing somewhere in the little terraced house, and no doubt was a vital component, which was why the entity had been so panicked when he had picked it up.

The cat's strange-smelling diarrhoea clinched it.

It wasn't diarrhoea at all, but some kind of strange discharge from the entity's equally extraterrestrial pet. It was, Henry thought, significant that he had not actually been allowed to see the "cat".

Now Alan Evans's murder fell into place too. The hapless trainspotter had obviously got equally close to the entity, and, like Henry himself, discovered its terrible secret. As soon as the creature had realised he might go to the authorities, it had ambushed him and silenced him for ever. What if it had his address from Findafuck as well? Henry shuddered. He was clearly in the deadliest danger.

Yet, at the same time he was quietly delighted with himself. The "little grey cells" had not let him down. What had looked like an obvious chance killing had led him to the greatest plot in the history of the universe, since the creature was clearly the advance scout for an invasion force.

But what could he do to save the human race? He couldn't just go and tell Hogg. Hogg was an old-fashioned provincial policeman, and simply wouldn't believe him. No, what he needed to do was break into the alien's house, and confiscate any extraterrestrial material as evidence. At the same time, there was a fair chance a copy of the invasion plans might be lurking in a drawer in the kitchen or somewhere.

His heart pounding, he dressed, went to his car, and drove into Bletchley. Parking up, he headed purposefully for Paddock Lane to stake out the house until the alien left. As he was walking up a neighbouring street, a very attractive auburn-haired woman in a business suit passed him in the opposite direction. "She looks interesting," thought Henry, and for a moment was tempted to abandon his quest and follow her. But duty got the better of him, and he headed inexorably towards his date with destiny.

When he arrived at Paddock Lane, it was only to find that…

but hang on, Henry's right. That woman does look interesting, doesn't she? Shall we follow her and see what she's doing, instead of going on with this silly tale of alien transvestite murderers? You don't agree? Well, tough titty, because this is my novel, and if you're read this far chances are you've bought it already, so I don't really need to humour you any longer.

The smart young woman made her way to a nearby pub, the Aardvark And Kettledrum, and on entering it was greeted by quizzical and admiring looks from the male clientele. Slightly embarrassed, she quickly found her colleagues and sat down with them. They, too, looked her up and down with ill-concealed interest and carnal lust.

In case you are thinking the lady is a prostitute and the blokes are her clients, not so; she is in fact a Director of Clambeard Homes (Southern) Ltd., and the sexist pigs are her fellow board members. They have arranged an impromptu lunchtime meeting away from the office, because Clambeard is faced by a serious…

*What? What? You're saying I abandoned the Henri LaFarge story because I couldn't think of an ending for it? You cheeky twat! Here's an ending for you: Brenda discovers Henry rummaging through her stuff, admits she is just a common-or-garden transsexual, and has him arrested for breaking and entering. Too boring? OK, here's another. Brenda apprehends him mid-rummage, but **is** an alien, and promptly kills him by ingesting him through her anal orifice. Instead of launching a full-blown invasion, the extraterrestrials decide to take over the world by stealth, and create a race of characterless, grinning Stepford Wives-type creatures to infiltrate global governments. One of them ends up running the UK on 1st May 1997.*

Now, if you'll kindly stop interrupting, I was about to say that Clambeard is faced by a serious threat to its public image from an elderly lady named Agnes LaChèvre.

Part Three: Spank.

Chapter One
A Load Of Bollards.

The desk of the executive personal assistant to the Chairman and Chief Executive of Clambeard Holdings plc, third largest construction firm in the UK, featured two telephones. The black one was for internal calls and the red one the direct outside line, whose number was issued only to a select few people. Unusually, it was the red one that was now ringing.

"Good morning, Clambeard, Chairman's Office," said Maureen Davis (*for 'twas she*) politely.

"Mr. Bollard, please." It was a thin, reedy voice, full of accusation.

Mrs. Davis closed her eyes in a moment's silent agony. "I'm sorry, Mrs. – er – LaChèvre, but *Sir Roddy* is not available at the moment. As I've told you before, he isn't really the person you need anyway. You should take this matter up with the Managing Director of Clambeard Homes Southern, although I really don't think there's anything to be resolved."

"That's what you said last time," retorted Agnes LaChèvre. "But you won't win. You're not going to harass me out of my home to build your filthy estate. You may have frightened the others off, but I'm made of stronger stuff. I was a WAAF in the war, you know."

"Mrs. LaChèvre, for the final time, no-one is trying to harass you out of your home. As you well know, we're not building anything within 20 miles of you."

"I've seen the ads, young lady, the ads. Copthorne Grove – 24 luxury executive homes at Copthorne Close, Shoreham. Only you won't be building anything unless you can make me move."

"Mrs. LaChèvre, that's Copthorne Close at Shoreham in Kent. You live at Copthorne Close in Shoreham-by-Sea in West Sussex. Now if you'll please excuse me, I'm rather busy."

"You haven't heard the last of this," declaimed the old lady. "I'll be looking for compensation for mental distress. Lots of it! And if you don't leave me alone, I'll set my son-in-law's dog Donald onto you!"

"And is Donald a very fierce dog, Mrs. LaChèvre?"

"Well, he knows the law, if that's what you mean! Now, good day to you."

Maureen Davis lowered the receiver in bafflement, and picked up the internal line.

Sir Roddy Bollard, thirty-seventh richest man in the UK, was not in a good mood. A small, wiry man with close-cropped dark hair and little thin-rimmed glasses, he was intently studying a typed letter with an expression midway between sorrow and fury.

Typical, he ruminated, typical. You heard so much about industrialists being encouraged to put something back into the community, then when you offered to do something for somebody, they simply smacked you in the mouth by way of thanks. Once again, he read the letter:

> "Dear Mr. Bollard
> ### Re: Chastisement Consultant
> I regret I must decline your offer to act as a Chastisement Consultant to this school. Notwithstanding that you clearly stated you would not require payment for these services, and would even make a six-figure donation to the College by way of goodwill, I can assure you that none of our girls require a good caning.
>
> Even if they did, we would be capable of handling this ourselves – and I do not agree that it would be necessary for their knickers to be removed whilst such punishment took place.
>
> You are clearly a very disturbed little man, and if I hear from you again, I shall pass your correspondence on to Sussex Police. And if you are thinking of paying us a visit, don't. As you may be aware, Roedean has electric fences all around and 24-hour guard dog patrols, as this was felt to be safer for the male population of Brighton.
>
> Yours sincerely,
> Zelda Baker, Headmistress.

PS" – this bit was handwritten – "*I cannot accede to your other request for photographs of spankings, as such pictures are sent directly to Men Only in return for funds for the College Chapel Restoration Project. Only joking, ZB.*"

The miserable, sour-faced old bitch! thought Sir Roddy, putting down the letter. She was probably a lesbian anyway, who took pleasure in undressing fifth form girls in her office, right down to their black leather bras and panties, then licking the sweat from their heaving shoulders, before picking up a good, old-fashioned, long-handled oak hairbrush, and placing it smartly in…

The telephone rang, which was probably just as well for the sake of his straining *(or should that be staining?)* trousers. Abandoning this pleasant fantasy, he picked it up and said perfunctorily, "Bollard."

"Sir Roddy, I've had Mrs. LaChèvre on the phone. She's still on about this harassment nonsense. God alone knows how she got the direct line number."

"That damn fool Jaqzi Calhoun must have given it to her. Let's hope she goes away. By the way, has the headmistress of Benenden replied to my letter yet?"

"No, Sir Roddy, and somehow I don't think she will."

"Damn. Damn. What does a little courtesy cost, after all? Anyway, what do you think that wretched LaChèvre woman is likely to do next?"

"Well, if I was her, Sir Roddy, I'd take it up with my MP."

Sir John Shertliffe-Tor MP was on the telephone, but not to Mrs. LaChèvre. Instead he seemed to be practising his lines for an amateur dramatic production, or suchlike.

"So I thought I'd stand and up say, 'Is my right honourable friend the Prime Minister aware that in my very own constituency, as many as two new job vacancies have been created by Billy Butler's Biscuits, to bake their fabulous range of chocolate digestives, almond shortbreads, gingerbread fingers and world-famous frangipane cookies, prices for which start from as little as 8p per packet?'" There was a long pause. "You want me to get your slogan 'Billy Butler bakes a better biscuit' in there somewhere? Well, OK, but that'll be another £50, I'm afraid." Another pause. "No, really, it's no problem. He who pays the piper and all that. I can accept payment by Access, Visa, American Express, bank transfer, postal order or cheque. If you send a cheque, please allow seven days for clearance, so the question won't get asked until a week Tuesday. Thank you, Mr. Butler, and goodbye."

Almost as soon as he had put down the phone, the door opened and his secretary came in. "Such a nice man, that Billy Butler," she said gaily. "Always pays his bills ever so promptly. Now then, Sir John, I've had a call from that LaChèvre woman. About the Clambeard business."

"Oh yes – I was wanting to speak to her," said Sir John grimly, his white moustache bristling with fury and the sweat standing out on his bald brow. "Making an appointment to see me at my constituency surgery, and then not turning up.

Pah! Anyone would think I'm in service to my bloody constituents."

"Well, Sir John, she did say she couldn't find the library. In fact, she insisted that Shoreham Library isn't in Snetterton Road at all."

"Course it is, the silly old loon. It's been there for the last thirty years. So what does the old trout want me to do?"

"She wondered if you wouldn't mind having a word with the Managing Director of Clambeard Homes Southern. He's an Irish-Indian gentleman named Mr. Jaqzi Calhoun. Think of it, Sir John – it'll be very good for your public image, helping out an old lady."

"Sod Jaqzi Calhoun."

"No, Sir John, that wouldn't be so good for your image, although I'm told he's very good-looking."

The MP laughed. "No, I meant I'd ring Roddy Bollard direct, as I know the chap. Why, what did you think I meant?"

His secretary smiled. "Oh nothing, Sir John, nothing. It really doesn't matter."

Roddy Bollard's brow was furrowed in concentration as he tried to think of a witty retort to the Roedean headmistress's letter. Maybe some joke about not needing a guard dog when there was a vicious old dog like her on the premises anyway, but then he remembered her threat about the police and thought better of it. Before he could put down his pencil and paper, the phone rang.

"Sir John Shertliffe-Tor, MP for Shoreham,"

said Maureen Davis.

"Bugger it," said Sir Roddy Bollard.

"Yes, he usually does," said Mrs. Davis, and put through the call.

"John! Wonderful to hear from you," said Sir Roddy, with false bonhomie. "Haven't heard from you in… must be four or five years… such a shame."

"And I haven't heard from *you* since Home fired me from the housing team and put me back on the back benches. Still haven't forgiven him for that."

"Yes," said Sir Roddy, "I remember that little blip in your political career."

"Can't be helped, old chap, can't be helped. Don't think I was ever cut out for the Cabinet, anyway. And Vaseline gave me a very lucrative directorship because it raised their profile so much."

"Good man," said Sir Roddy perfunctorily. "So how are you keeping, anyway?"

"Oh, mustn't grumble. I say, you must be very excited about Saturday week." There was a long silence from Bollard. "You know, the big performance. It's not every day Alfredo Tossa comes to London to perform *La Traviata*. Bet you booked your seat months ago."

Now Sir Roddy remembered. When John Shertliffe-Tor had been a junior housing minister under Macmillan, Sir Roddy had pretended to share his passion for opera in an attempt to curry favour. This had led to some of the most buttock-numbingly boring evenings of his life. When it came to culture, Bollard much preferred a good school play, although he spent most of his time watching the audience.

"Yes, old chap, expect I'll see you there. Now, something tells me this isn't a social call."

"Bullseye, dear boy. Does the name Agnes LaChèvre mean anything to you?"

"Yes, she's the loony who says we're trying to force her out of her home. I've had it up to here with her."

Shertliffe-Tor was solicitous. "Well, it does sound like she's tried to be reasonable, Rod, old boy. Says she's offered you her house, admittedly at slightly above the market value –"

"About ten times the market value," said Sir Roddy.

"– but you turned her down, although you'll clearly need her land. You *are* building at Copthorne Close, aren't you?"

"Well, yes, but…"

"Word of warning, old chap. Try to settle it with her out of court. Widow being harassed out of her home by big building firm, could be very messy. And that's even before the government gets involved. Between you and me, Mr. Major takes a very dim view of this sort of thing."

Sir Roddy was confused. "I'm sorry, who?"

"Mr. Major, old chap. The PM."

"But I thought Edward Heath was Prime Minister."

There was a long, embarrassed pause. Finally,

Shertliffe-Tor ventured, *sotto voce*, "Tell me, old fellow, what year's this bally novel set in?"

"1972, old chap."

"Blast! My agent said it was '92! If he'd told me it was '72, I wouldn't have agreed to do it. I hate these historical dramas. The script's flimsier than a French tart's fancy knickers, as well."

"Mmm," sympathised Sir Roddy. "My character's not exactly well-rounded, either."

"Quite, quite. Must be very difficult for you – all that schoolgirl stuff."

Sir Roddy was suddenly suspicious. "What do you mean by that?"

"Come, come, old fellow, everybody in Equity knows you're as bent as a seven pound note."

"Is that so, ducky? Well, let me just say that your performance as a parliamentary poofter is surprisingly convincing."

"Well, I had a pretty good rôle model to work from, didn't I?"

"Right, in a minute I'm going to come up there and scratch your…"

The other telephone rang on Sir Roddy's desk. It was Maureen Davis. "I've just had the author on the line," she said crossly, "and he's fed up with you two queens wrangling. In fact, he says if you don't stop it, he'll write a scene in which a giant woodpecker swoops down and eats your genitals for breakfast."

"Remind the bastard he's getting paid by the word," said Sir Roddy, "so all our bickering is paying for his schoolgirls."

(Author's note: Sir Roddy is lying. I do not have any schoolgirls, nor any interest in schoolgirls. It is Sir Roddy Bollard, who is a fictional character and does not exist, who likes schoolgirls, and not me. It is also Sir Roddy, not me, who likes spanking schoolgirls. Just thought I'd make that clear in case there's any police officers reading. If so, good work, I really support you boys in blue, you do a sterling job, and could I ask you to recommend this book to your desk sergeant down the nick, the gaoler, any members of CID who may be hanging around, and also any members of the criminal underworld you happen to know. I've got a mortgage to pay, unlike you with your all-expenses-met section house. PS: That last remark was not intended as criticism. Sorry. Thank you for listening.)

Sir Roddy put the phone down and returned to his conversation with the MP. "Yes, let's not fall out, old fellow. This *is* a bloody awful book, but it'll pay a few bills until the pantomime season begins. I feel more sorry for you, really – playing an MP who accepts bribes to ask parliamentary questions. I mean, it's just not realistic, is it?"

"Well, not in 1972, dear boy. 100 years ago, maybe. Anyway, must be going – see you down the Swiss Cottage And Arresting Officer for a quick half."

"No hang on, old fellow, there's more in the script. I'm supposed to tell you that you're the MP for Shoreham & Otford in Kent and Mrs.

LaChèvre lives in Shoreham-by-Sea in Sussex."

"Seems a pretty flimsy joke to me to build a book around, that's all I can say. Be seeing you." And with that, the MP crisply put down the phone.

Chapter Two
Blue Tit Blues.

Agnes LaChèvre carefully counted the numbers of each of the buildings until she came to number 101. As expected, this was a smart, modern office block, one of the few standing out from the West End department stores on Oxford Street.

Oddly, the brass plaques made no mention of Clambeard Holdings; perhaps they had had so much controversy over the years that they did not want to advertise their presence. Well, that was nothing compared to the controversy that would befall them today! Whatever, all she had to do now was wait for the press to arrive and make her protest.

It was a cold spring day and Aggie shivered. Periodically, she checked her watch. Eleven... then ten past... then twenty-two minutes past. Typical of the bloody media! They'd seemed excited enough when she had told them about her problems with Clambeard, and dropped heavy hints that she would be staging a spectacular protest at their office, but then they couldn't even be bothered to turn up on time. Oh well. She would give it until twelve, and if they hadn't appeared then, she would do the protest anyway. Somebody was bound to notice.

Every so often, a car would draw up outside, and she would expect it to be a newspaper reporter or a TV crew, but the promised media presence was conspicuous by its absence. Finally, at five past twelve, she decided to get on with it.

First, she unfurled a large, gaudy home-made banner proclaiming "Clambeard can't take away my home", then she yelled, "They can have the shirt off my back, but they can't make me move," and began to perform a striptease.

As the heavy camel coat slipped off her shoulders, she shivered. When she divested herself of her checked woollen cardigan, she trembled. When it came time to remove her white lacy blouse, she paused, then steeled herself and did so. This revealed a bizarre, old-fashioned brassière, a peculiar contraption of whalebone, steel and voluminous folds of discoloured cream material. A workman driving by in his truck whistled. Aggie responded only by slipping off the bra, revealing unbelievably ancient and pendulous breasts that sagged sadly towards the pavement like a drunkard hit by the cold night air. Finally, she removed her skirt and tights. As she stood, wearing only her thermal long-johns, wondering whether to complete the publicity stunt, a small man clutching a large camera rushed up.

"Hold it right there, love," he said in a Glaswegian drawl, before taking photographs of her from all angles, concentrating especially on her breasts. "That's lovely… lovely. What's your name, love?"

"Are you from the media?" she enquired haughtily.

"Naw, I'm just a pervert." The man gave a wheezy laugh. "Only kidding. I'm Jock McBairn from *The Sun*."

Aggie fixed him with a stern glare. "You were due here over an hour ago."

McBairn shook his head. "No, love. Wasn't due here at all. Lucky I was passing. I was down at Clambeard's offices to cover some protest, only the woman never showed."

A chill of fear added to the cold Aggie was already feeling. "But these are Clambeard's offices, aren't they? 101 Oxford Street?"

"No, love. You want 101 New Oxford Street. It's about a mile-and-a-half down the road."

Aggie began to dress hurriedly. "And were there other media people there?"

"It was like a circus, love, like a circus."

"Oh God. I'd better get down there fast."

McBairn laughed. "You do that, love. Let's hope the woman who invited the reporters doesn't show, though – they'll tear her to pieces for keeping them waiting."

Aggie reconsidered quickly. "Well, maybe I ought to be getting home."

"And I'd better be getting back to the office," said McBairn. "Over an hour I was standing outside that building, and the only person who went in was some scary lady carrying a hockey stick."

"A hockey stick?"

"Yes, said she was the headmistress of Benenden, and wanted a word with Sir Roddy Bollard. Anyway, must be going, Mrs. – er…"

"LaChèvre. Agnes LaChèvre."

"Well, thanks, Mrs. LaChèvre. I'll be seeing you."

A thought suddenly struck Aggie. "If this isn't Clambeard, then whose offices have I been stripping in front of?"

"Well, if memory serves me correctly it's the British Psychiatric Association, but don't quote me on that." And with that McBairn disappeared back into the crowd, his grubby macintosh flapping in the wind.

At that moment, the door opened, and a strange little man wearing purple-and-yellow checked trousers emerged.

"What a vile day!" he said, in a weird sing-song manner, then to Aggie: "I thought your performance was really interesting… from a clinical perspective. Will you come inside and talk about it?"

"Oh, I don't know, Mr…"

"Doctor. Dr. Bacon. I'm Director-General of Graylingwell psychiatric hospital in West Sussex, and I'm up here for a little conference. But I've got a few minutes spare, so I'd love to talk to you…"

Why not? thought Aggie, as she went into the building with the strange man. After all, he could hear all about her struggle with the evil forces of capitalism at Clambeard.

Chapter Three
Saggy Aggie In The Soaraway Sun.

"Oh, Mum." Agnes LaChèvre's daughter Patsy put down the copy of *The Sun* with a mournful sigh. "You've really made a fool of yourself, haven't you?"

"Can I see?" said her mother, reaching over for the paper.

And indeed, Mrs. LaChèvre had made quite something of a splash. Most of pages four and five had been devoted to her, dwarfing the insignificant byline "Heath says nuclear war possible before twenty-first century".

The exposé featured a large picture of Agnes topless, with the banner headline *"We're just mad about saggy Aggie"*, and the copy read:

"Way-hey! Visitors to London's posh Oxford Street got an eyeful yesterday when randy grannie Agnes LaChèvre, 67, stripped off in full view of our cameraman. This was apparently intended as some sort of protest, but no-one we noticed was protesting about the spectacle, even though Aggie's assets have suffered from the effects of gravity.

Following her amazing striptease, Aggie had a brief conversation with Dr. Colin Bacon, the controversial director of Graylingwell mental hospital. Dr. Bacon told our reporter: "This lady is clearly suffering from repressed childhood neuroses causing her to seek the limelight. In my opinion, she is clearly very disturbed, and in need of professional help. If she comes to me for treatment, I guarantee she'll be as sane as I am in six weeks." Dr. Bacon went on to say: "Have you noticed a really cosmic vibe about London today?" and "Do you know if there are any fountains around here, so I can go and pray to one?"

Well, your soaraway Sun *doesn't care what crackpot Bacon thinks: we just love saggy old Aggie! So come on granddads, get yourself an eyeful. WAY-HEY!"*

Agnes swallowed hard. "Well, it's not quite what I hoped for. But I suppose any publicity is good publicity. I bet that Mr. Bollard won't believe his eyes when he sees this."

Roddy Bollard put down the newspaper with a deeply concerned expression. "She's mad," he said, "utterly mad. I tell you, I'm terrified. Someone that unstable could come stalking me at any minute. I'll have to meet her face-to-face and sort it all out."

"That could be dangerous," said Maureen Davis solicitously.

"Yes, but it's the only way. I'll head down to Shoreham-by-Sea tomorrow morning and confront her."

"No, Sir Roddy. Tomorrow morning you're having the operation to remove the hockey stick. You'll have to wait until Wednesday."

"OK, Wednesday, then. And whilst I'm down there, I'll make a little detour to Roedean. It's only a few miles away."

"In that case, Sir Roddy, I'll book you in for a further emergency operation on Thursday."

And with that, his ever-efficient personal assistant left the room.

Chapter Four
Schoolgirls Ahoy!

Shoreham-by-Sea is a pleasant, relaxing town, roughly halfway between Worthing and Brighton. Its main asset is a very pleasant but tiny historic centre, set around the beautiful St. Mary de Haura church. This is surrounded by a few extremely attractive ancient cottages, all of which fetch substantial prices. *(Note to Shoreham Confederation of Estate Agents: all cheques should be made payable to "R. Falk".)*

One of these cottages turned out to be the home of Agnes LaChèvre, and Bollard made for it purposefully. When he knocked on the door, it was not Mrs. LaChèvre herself, but a smart, military-style man with white hair and a short moustache, clad in a blazer and yacht club tie, who answered the door.

(Author's note: When I said he was clad in a blazer and yacht club tie, I didn't mean that's all he was wearing. The bloke also has on underpants, a white shirt, a pair of cavalry twill slacks, and shoes and socks. I didn't mean to imply he was some kind of sexual pervert who answers the door naked from the waist down. Although if that image sexually excites you, and makes you feel happier about the

money you've paid for this book, then I take back the foregoing. If half-naked old men turn you on, then hey, I'm not judgmental. Just don't think you're getting an invitation to any of my parties.)

"Is Mrs. LaChèvre in?" asked Sir Roddy politely.

"Indeed she is, but she's cooking," said the elderly man affably. "I am Colonel Giles LaChèvre. May I help you?"

"But I thought… Mrs. LaChèvre always said she was a widow."

"In that case," said Colonel Giles gravely, "you must be Sir Roddy Bollard." He closed the door behind him, walked forward and laid his hands on Sir Roddy's lapel. For a moment, Sir Roddy thought he might strike him, but Colonel Giles continued, "My dear fellow, I owe you the most copious apology. I understand my wife has led you a terribly merry dance, accusing you of attempting to harry us out of our home."

"Well, yes," said Sir Roddy, nonplussed.

"You see, I've been away in India on a reunion tour with my old regiment for three months. My wife took the opportunity to attempt a little – er – money-making scheme. You see, old fellow, she's really under the most dreadful pressure. So when she saw in the *Evening Standard* that you were building in Shoreham, Kent, in a road with the same name as this one, that made her come up with the idea."

"What idea?"

"Well, to offer you our house at ten times the

market value, and to pretend you were attempting to get us out at a cut price when you didn't buy. She was hoping you'd give in and pay up to avoid the bad publicity. I know it's technically blackmail, but you've got to accept that she was absolutely desperate to escape."

"Escape?" said Sir Roddy. "But it's so delightful here. So lovely and peaceful."

"For now, old chap, for now." Colonel Giles looked him directly in the eye. "A plague is about to descend upon our house, old man."

"I'm sorry?"

"Well, can you imagine this place crawling with teenage schoolgirls, laughing and shrieking, hanging around outside the shops looking to pick up boys?"

"Oh yes," said Sir Roddy dreamily, as a lump began to form in his trousers.

"Well, we couldn't stand the bally idea. However the council gave those people permission to construct the largest girls' public school in Europe I have no idea. Some money must have changed hands. Anyway, we decided to sell up. But so did everyone else around here, and of course nobody would buy except at a knockdown price. That's when my wife came up with the idea to get us out with a profit."

Sir Roddy was desperate to speak, but Colonel Giles continued without a pause. "Anyway, thanks for being so understanding, old chap. I promise we won't pester you again. In any case, we've decided to stay and fight. No school's going to drive us out of our home. All the neighbours have taken their houses off the market as well." He laughed. "Apparently, my wife asked you for £80,000 for this place. Outrageous! It's only worth £8000! Anyway, it's good to have met you. I'm sure we won't meet again."

And with that, he shook Sir Roddy's hand, and went back inside, closing the door behind him.

Sir Roddy's lip was beginning to tremble. "I'll give you £80,000 for the house," he whimpered. "I'll give you £800,000 for it. Please, please, please sell me your house. I want to live in Shoreham more than anywhere else in the world…"

But the door remained closed, as Sir Giles went off to enjoy the scones his wife had just baked, and Sir Roddy slid down the door, weeping hysterically.

An elderly couple, walking down the other side of the road, regarded him quizzically.

"What's going on there?" said the wife, puzzled. "Is that fellow all right? Or do you do think he's on drugs or something?"

"None of our business if he is," replied her husband, hurrying on. "Anyway, I reckon there's a hidden camera somewhere round here. I should think this is a stunt for the TV or something."

"It'd have to be a kids' programme, then," concluded his wife, "the way the bloke's overacting."

Part Four: Jugs.

Chapter One
Muffy And His Furry Friends
In The Land Of Muff.

The offices of Hande-Shandie International, purveyors of innovative quality children's television, were to be found in a smart but slightly austere grey office building overlooking Regent's Park. Don't bother looking for it – it's not there any more. *(That's a reference to my favourite film of all time – do you know the one I mean?)*

David Peters and his fiancée Sarah Stoner had little trouble finding the building using their shiny new A-Z, and felt slightly overwhelmed as they entered through the massive banks of smoked glass doors, set above wide, sweeping marble steps. Inside the cavernous reception, giant stills of Hande-Shandie's most famous productions were everywhere: above the reception desk, above the lifts, even incorporated into the huge clock that proudly announced it was twenty past ten.

They had to wait a couple of minutes at the desk before a slightly severe middle-aged woman, in a crisp black dress, came over to see them.

"Good morning," she said. "And how may I help you?"

David did not like her somewhat imperious attitude. "Tell Mr. Shandie David Peters and Sarah

Stoner are here to see him," he said loudly, and with some pride. "We have a *personal appointment* to discuss a new programme concept."

"Of course you do," said the woman. "Thursday is always 'Talent Day'." She spoke the words as though they were an insult. "You're the half past ten slot, and you will have twenty minutes with Mr. Shandie. Unfortunately, he is running a few minutes late, so please join the queue over there." With this, she gestured to a line of scruffy stragglers, incongruously clogging up the otherwise pristine reception.

Crestfallen, David and Sarah shuffled over to join them, muttering sourly about how they had been deceived into thinking they had been given a personal appointment, and how twenty minutes was clearly insufficient to explain the epochal television concept they had brought with them. Evidently, they were in for a bit of a wait.

It was, in fact, ten past eleven before they were shown into Bob Shandie's impressive office, whose floor-to-ceiling windows commanded spectacular views over the park. Shandie was younger and thinner than they had imagined, a friendly-looking man with a mobile, animated face, a shock of prematurely grey-white hair, and a wiry frame. Today he was wearing a single-breasted light grey suit, pale shirt, and a vivid "cartoon character" tie.

As soon as they entered, he advanced with a broad smile and an outstretched hand. "Come in, come in, make yourselves at home. Sorry we're running late, but you know how it is. You just can't get some people to shut up."

David and Sarah smiled wanly, and Shandie noticed that they were extremely nervous. He looked them up and down in a professional manner. David was a good-looking young man of about thirty, with firm features and dark, wavy hair. Sarah was an attractive woman in her early twenties, with long auburn hair, and a fine, full-breasted figure. She was not, Shandie noticed suddenly, wearing a bra, and her nipples could be clearly seen straining against the tight yellow T-shirt.

Breaking his stare, Shandie invited them to sit down, and continued, "Before you tell me about your concept, I'd like to get to know you for a couple of minutes. What made you choose Hande-Shandie to share your ideas with?"

"Well," said David, "we've always admired you immensely." Sarah nodded vigorously. "I mean, most people think of the great children's TV producers as being American – Hanna-Barbera and people like that – but for us Hande-Shandie are the only people that count."

Shandie nodded graciously. "That's very kind. And which of our programmes is your favourite?"

"Oh, it would have to be *Skydog And Webcat*."

"Yes," interjected Sarah. "Such a clever idea, to combine a children's cartoon and a consumer rights show in a single programme."

"Yes," said Shandie. "We won a lot of awards for that concept. So, which episode did you like best?"

"Well, my personal favourite," David pondered for a moment, "was the one where Webcat's new video failed to record *Match Of The Day*, so Skydog flew over to Eindhoven and nuked the Philips factory."

Shandie got up, and wandered over to the far wall, where a giant picture of the cartoon duo was proudly displayed. Skydog was, as usual, in his Fokker biplane, leather helmet and goggles encasing his head, and a machine gun within reach of his hairy paws. Slender, grey Webcat, meanwhile, was as normal spinning a gossamer web, and probably bemoaning the low standard of service he had received at the supermarket that morning.

"And you, er – Sarah. Is that your favourite episode as well?"

"Oh yes, I like that as well. But I also liked the one with the patio doors." Sarah had clearly done her homework, as she began to quote directly from the script. "*'So,' said Skydog grimly, 'you mean to say that your firm aren't members of the Glass and Glazing Federation, which means that my friend Webcat's new patio doors aren't unconditionally guaranteed for a full ten years?' Struggling against the ropes that bound him to his chair, the hapless double glazing salesman began stammering out excuses about how he would personally guarantee the doors, but it was too late. Skydog's machine gun rat-a-tat-tatted, and filled the man's chest with red gaping holes. 'He won't be ripping anybody else off,' said Skydog, and he and Webcat laughed until they cried.*"

"Very impressive," said Shandie, returning to his seat, "and now let's see whether you've come up with the next *Skydog And Webcat*, shall we?"

"We were just wondering…" said David, "whether you could tell us a bit about your own professional background? You see, you're sort of a hero of ours."

Shandie checked his watch doubtfully. "Well, OK," he said, "but we'll have to be quick. There's not much to tell, really. After I left school, I was a publisher's reader, then I roadied for a couple of bands, then I made my way into artist management. I was personal manager to one of the top pop acts of the sixties – Billy The Bedouin And His Ay-rabs."

David and Sarah looked blank.

"Yes, well, lot of water under the bridge since then." Shandie again walked to the far wall, and pointed out a signed black-and-white photograph. It featured five teenagers with their faces unconvincingly blacked up, wearing Arab head-dresses. "Oh, yes. They were a fine band. Missed out on the big time by a hair's breadth. They played with all the stars, of course. My proudest moment was when they were seventeenth on the bill to The Beatles at the Skegness Locarno in May 1964. All the girls were screaming when they came on stage…"

"What were they screaming?" asked Sarah, impressed.

"Well, mainly it was 'John', 'Paul', 'Ringo' and 'George'," recalled Shandie, "although one or two were shouting 'Piss off, we want The Beatles', but it was a wonderful night, wonderful."

"Did they get any records out?" asked David.

Shandie laughed. "Did they release any records? They had a smash hit, young man – January 1966, with *Fatty Fatima*. Number 17, and eight weeks in the top fifty." Very unexpectedly, he drew himself up to his full height and began to sing:

> *"She's got a tum like a camel-skin drum*
> *And she makes my heart go b-boom – yeah!"*

There was a long, embarrassed silence, broken only when David said, "Oh yeah, I think I do know it. Did they have any other hits?"

Shandie shook his head. "*Shakin' Sheikh* only just missed the Top 50, but after that they couldn't get arrested. Problem was, the critics didn't like them. Said they were nothing but a poor imitation of Sam The Sham And The Pharaohs, which is ridiculous, as they were a totally different concept. Still, what the fuck do critics know?"

"And where's Billy today?" said David. "Sunning himself at an oasis somewhere, no doubt."

"What, Bill Arkwright? No, he took over his father's frozen food business in Preston. Anyway, back to the story, we're running out of time. After the band split up, I met Les Hande at a showbusiness party, and we decided progressive children's TV was the way of the future. We set up in March 1968, with four staff to begin with.

Look at us now – 230 staff, and our programmes are syndicated all over the world. Of course, it's lucky that *Skydog And Webcat* was our first production. But we've never forgotten the need to come up with new ideas, which is why I hold these auditions every Thursday. *Ali Butt And His Fishy Friends* came out of these sessions. Anyway, enough of my yakkin'…" – *that's another reference to my all-time favourite film, in case you didn't get the first one* – "let's see what you've got."

In a few seconds, he would realise just how prophetic these words were.

"Right," said David, suddenly businesslike. "For the full effect, we'll need the office darkened. Would you mind closing those blinds whilst I turn off the lights?"

"OK," said Shandie doubtfully. "It's not a magic act, is it? We do try to make it very clear that we're not interested in magic acts."

"No, not at all," said David, rummaging for something in his briefcase. "This is a really fresh and exciting children's TV concept. I think you're going to love it. It's mainly inspired by the Black Theatre Of Prague, and it'll be as cheap to make as *Fingerbobs*."

(Author's note: For those readers too young to remember these programmes, allow me to explain. The Black Theatre Of Prague was a sort of primitive animation in which scissors and other household objects were suspended in front of a black screen and made to 'dance' and perform using bits of cotton.

It wasn't exactly Manga Animation, let's put it that way. Fingerbobs *was a programme for young children in which a Jewish-looking hippie told stories, which he illustrated with amateurish finger puppets. The production budget for the show must have been about 50 pence – in old money. Actually, no, the budget was probably enormous, and the Jewish bloke most likely trousered the cash, and then spent 50 pence on the programme. Anyway, I digress.)*

"*Et voilà,*" said David, with a flourish. "*Son et lumière.*"

And with that, he switched on the torches he was holding to reveal Sarah standing topless, her magnificent young breasts gleaming in the creamy-yellow light. By switching on one torch or the other, or both simultaneously, David could illuminate either of Sarah's breasts at will, or both together.

Bob Shandie swallowed hard, unable to believe his eyes.

"Hello, children," said David in a patronising voice. "And welcome to *Juggy And His Friend*. Say hello to the children, Juggy."

Sarah wiggled her left breast and creased up the nipple – without even touching it, so this was clearly her party piece – whilst David called out "Hello, sir!" in a high, silly voice.

"And now let's say hello to Juggy's Friend." The right breast went through exactly the same routine. David turned to Shandie. "Of course, you really need music to get the full picture, but this should give you the idea."

"Yes," said Shandie. "Oh yes, it certainly does."

"Now then, Juggy," David was back to the patronising voice. "Have you been a good boy since we last saw you?" And then, in the high-pitched voice, "Yes, sir!" The left breast wobbled up and down, as though nodding. "And Juggy's Friend, have you been a good boy too?" Another vigorous wobble. "You haven't been poking your LBNs into other people's business, have you?" Now the breasts shook from side to side. "No, sir!" they chorused.

Bob Shandie interrupted. "I beg your pardon, but what exactly is an LBN?"

"Oh, I'm sorry," said Sarah. "We should have explained. LBNs are what Juggy and his Friend call their nipples – short for Little Brown Noses. It's what they use to see the world, you see."

"Yes, yes, of course it is. How silly of me."

"So what do you think?" said David, turning off the torches, and switching the main lights back on. "Innovative or what?"

"Well, yes, it's certainly original, but…"

"You see, this isn't just some empty gimmick. We've worked really hard on the characterisation. Juggy and his friend are going to be really mischievous – sort of everyman characters, with whom the children will really be able to identify."

"Oh yes," interjected Sarah. "They'll get up to some terrible scrapes, because they're really inquisitive."

"Fine," said Bob Shandie, "but I really don't think we can use this."

David and Sarah looked at him in a stunned silence.

"And why not?" said David archly.

"Bare breasts on pre-school television," said Shandie. "Just not on, I'm afraid."

"I'm not ashamed of my body," said Sarah – which, indeed, she was not, as she had made no attempt to get dressed. "And let's face it, it's nothing the kids won't have seen before. After all, they'll have been sucking their mothers' tits when they were babies."

"Ah, yes," said David dreamily. "Their eager infant mouths quickly finding the swollen, russet brown nipple, and expertly teasing it into erection. Their tongues probing and caressing, their delicate infant lips sucking, until their mother begins to emit long, slow groans of ecstasy as her breasts climax in a warm torrent of love-milk, exploding over the infant's grateful taste-buds like…"

Shandie held up his hand. "Yes, thank you, thank you, I get the picture. I'm sorry, but what you're proposing is impossible. No TV company would ever allow it."

"Well, I still think you're wrong," said David. "This would be the first kids' programme to appeal to the dads as well as the children."

"Ah," said Shandie. "That's a common misconception. You see, infants generally watch TV with their mothers rather than their fathers, and if the ladies wanted to see a pair of breasts, they'd just find a mirror. But in general…" he waved a hand airily. "Even if you took the breasts out of the equation, I still think the show is a little one-dimensional. Two characters and a voiceover are not enough to keep the modern child's interest."

David slapped his thigh. "I'm sorry, Mr. Shandie, but we've only shown you half the concept. There's plenty more characters to meet."

"Are there?" said Shandie, nervously.

"Oh, yes. For a start, there's Muffy the Muff. Show him, love." With that, Sarah began to hitch up her skirt. "And if that's still not enough, Nobby the Nob will put in the odd guest appearance – along with his neighbours."

"His neighbours?"

"Yes, his friends the Plums, who live at Numbers 1 and 2, The Bollocks."

Shandie made a shooing gesture. "Yes, yes, I've heard enough. Perhaps another time. I think this concept needs a lot more work before you visit us again, but thanks for coming."

David and Sarah left in an angry silence. The latter's clothing was still in disarray, which attracted odd looks from the staff. Shandie welcomed his next guest – a slim, bespectacled man in a pinstripe suit – whilst David and Sarah's mutterings of "Wanker!", "Boring old fart!" and "He's losing his touch – *Ali Butt And His Fishy Friends* was complete shit!" could be heard from down the corridor.

Chapter Two
Guernica Meets Farthing Wood.

"**S**orry about that," said Shandie, showing the dapper little man into his office. "As if I weren't running late enough already, I get those two trying to sell me the most ridiculous concept I ever heard. Sometimes I think I should discontinue these Thursday Talent Sessions, and do something constructive with the time."

"Yes," said the little man, settling himself down. "I quite understand."

"Now, then, Mr. – er – Lewis. Have you got any previous background in writing for children's TV?"

"In a nutshell, no." The pinstriped nerd looked genuinely downcast. "It's always been an interest of mine – not that I have any children, you understand. Too busy looking after my mother, you see, and my civil service job took up lots of my time. Never seemed to find the right woman, either. Even tried a couple of agencies."

"I'm told Findafuck are pretty good," said Shandie. "Apparently they can find a partner for anybody, but my wife won't let me find out."

The expected laughter did not materialise. "No, no, Findafuck was one of the ones I tried," said the little man earnestly. "They didn't find anybody for me, so that claim can't be true. Somebody should have a word with them, and make them change it."

"Well, yes, but that's hardly our…"

"No, I mean I'm not a man of strong views or anything, but these people, they're playing with people's feelings. I remember the day I joined, I was so excited…"

Shandie checked his watch. "Mr. Lewis, if you could just tell me about your…"

"I thought to myself, 'This is it, Norman Lewis! Your bachelor days are over!' Of course, Mother didn't know I'd joined. I don't suppose she would have been too pleased, me putting myself in danger like that. They say you get some very funny people in those clubs."

Bob Shandie was now regarding him with a fixed and very false smile. "Yes. Yes. I can quite believe that."

"I mean, I thought to myself, they'll find me a nice girl. Maybe a pretty blonde, about seventeen…"

"Seventeen?" Now he had got Shandie's full attention. "You thought you'd have a relationship with a seventeen-year-old?"

"Yes. Of course, I was a lot younger at the time…" Shandie relaxed and nodded. "Only in my early forties then. I mean, I'm not a fussy man – she'd have to have a good figure, but she didn't need to look like Twiggy."

"Mr. Lewis… Norman… if we could just get on to your script."

"I asked for my money back and everything. They wouldn't hear of it. The woman said I had abused their rules by putting in a silly request. Said I should have gone for a quiet, mature lady. I mean, what would I want with some middle-aged woman who's spent twenty years in a dead-end job and done nothing with her life?"

"Mr. Lewis, I am a busy man. If you don't get to the point, I shall have to ask you to…"

The little man leaped to his feet, shaking his fist in rage. "STOP INTERRUPTING ME!" he screamed at an earsplitting volume. Shandie flinched and looked left and right, to see whether a suitable weapon might present itself should the psychotic little man launch a physical assault. Only the telephone fitted the bill. That would do.

(Author's note to younger readers: telephones in the early seventies were very much bulkier and heavier than modern ones. If confronted by a dangerous psycho, possibly armed, do not engage him in combat with a trimphone. Or if you must, then strangle him with the cord.)

Several seconds of almost unbearable tension were broken when the little man lowered himself back into his seat. "Sorry about that, Mr. Shandie," he continued, in a normal voice. "I do appreciate your busy schedule, but I am getting rather tired of people not listening to what I have to say. Now, I have travelled all the way up from Warminster today, and if I ask you to give me a few more than the regulation twenty minutes, I don't think that's unreasonable."

His only response was a wide, patronising smile and a slight nod of the head.

"I'll be as quick as I can, I promise... anyway, where was I? Oh yes, I couldn't find a girlfriend, and Mother died two years ago, then in July I was made redundant, so I was just sitting around in this big, empty house, and I thought 'I know! I'll become a children's television writer!'" Shandie made no answer. The little man giggled. "Well, Mr. Shandie? Aren't you going to ask about my script?"

"Oh yes, yes, of course. Can you give me a brief idea of what your programme's about?"

"I can do better than that." Norman Lewis produced a sheaf of paper, covered in a weird childlike scrawl, from his briefcase. "I've written the entire pilot script. Let me read it to you."

"Oh God," said Shandie involuntarily.

"We may be here for an hour or so, so you may as well make yourself comfortable, Mr. Shandie. Now, you see, my programme is a story programme about animals. It's called *The Animals Of Hampton Dell*. It's a sort of story format, with watercolour illustrations, a bit like *Jackanory*."

(Author's note: For those readers too young to remember Jackanory, *chances are you are too young to be reading a book with lots of swear words like this one. So please stop immediately, and forget everything you have already read. Or, if you're browsing through this in a bookshop, then ignore what I've just said and buy the fucker anyway.)*

Shandie held up his hand. "Now I do hope you won't be offended, Mr. Lewis, but Hande-Shandie is in the business of cutting-edge television. What you're proposing might well appeal to children, but I'm afraid it doesn't have the originality we're looking for… although I'm sure it's terribly good."

Again that weird, falsetto giggle. "I'm not offended, Mr. Shandie. But wait till you hear this. There's quite a twist in the tale. In the tail, get it?" Falsetto giggle. "That was a pun, Mr. Shandie. 'In the tale' – and my programme's all about animals and their tails."

Shandie laughed perfunctorily. "Sidesplitting."

"Now then, this first episode is called *A Visit To Beeching's Farm*. I won't introduce you to the characters; you'll meet them as we go along."

"Fine," said Shandie, reflecting that the loon's babblings would at least give him a chance to catch up on his meditation.

"Are you sitting comfortably? Then we'll begin:

It was a beautiful bright day down at Hampton Dell. The sun was shining golder than a lock of Goldilocks's hair, and the sky was bluer than an uncut print of Emmanuelle. *It was a wonderful day to be alive, and the animals were dancing and gambolling with their furry friends.*

Everybody was just discussing what to do, when Billy the Badger piped up and said, "I'm hungry."

"Ooh, yes!" everybody cried. "We're hungry too!"

Everybody loved Billy the Badger because he was such a playful fellow, always getting up to mischief.

Then Christina the Chicken said, "You could always eat some grass, Billy."

"Ooh, I know," said Billy, "but I'm bored with grass. I could just fancy a nice, juicy green apple."

"So could I," said Vernon the Vole, "but we don't have any nice, juicy green apples. All we've got is grass."

"No," said Billy, "but there's plenty of lovely green apples up at Beeching's Farm."

Everybody gasped to hear such a naughty suggestion from such a little black-and-white badger.

"Come on, Billy," said Myfanwy the Mole, who, being Welsh, was a bit timid. "Isn't that rather dangerous? If the farmer catches us, won't he be very angry?"

"Well, he may be a bit cross," Billy pondered. "But after all, what can he do? Anyway, he's got to catch us first!"

After much discussion, all the friends agreed to go and find some apples. Even little Myfanwy, who would have been much happier making a tunnel underground.

Off they went, their little paws going pitter-pat over the warm ground. It was a very long walk to Beeching's Farm, more than one of the humans' miles, and everybody was exhausted by the time they got there.

"I don't know about you," said Billy, "but if I didn't need that apple before, I certainly do now."

Everyone agreed that they, too, were so hungry they could eat a whole treeful of apples. And there were lots of trees full of apples just beyond the barbed wire fence that marked the edge of Beeching's Farm.

"Through we go, and quietly now," said Billy, as one by one, our intrepid friends wriggled through gaps in the wire netting.

"So far, so good," said Christina the Chicken, who by now was really ravenous. "Let's eat!"

Billy bade her to hold back, and pointed out that stealth was of the utmost importance. So slowly, slowly they inched forward, until Vernon was able to shin up one of the trees, and bring down a glowing green apple for each of his friends.

"OK, let's go back home," said Billy indistinctly, his mouth filled by the huge apple. "Quietly now!"

But when they returned to the gap in the fence, our friends were in for a very big shock! For there was the farmer, and he wasn't looking at all pleased at seeing his prize apples being scrumped.

"Let's scarper!" said Billy, dropping his apple. "It's every man for himself."

And off they went, their little paws pitter-pattering, and the farmer's big boots going clomp-clomp-clomp as he chased after them, shouting and cursing as he went. With the farmer's big strides, he was gaining on the animals every second, and Billy's heart was beating so hard he thought it might explode.

But the animals were wily, and the farmer zig-zagged this way and that, not sure who he should chase or which of our furry friends to catch first. Finally, Billy gave up the chase and hid in a bush. Most of the other animals did the same, but poor old Christina the Chicken was a bit slow, and the farmer *caught her by her tail feathers and lifted her up.*

Did she squawk and did she cluck as the farmer held her tight and glared into her beady chicken eyes! "Dear, oh dear," thought Billy. "Christina's in for a right telling-off now!"

But the farmer seemed angrier than that, and produced a shiny, six-inch Bowie knife from his pocket, with a wicked silver blade. Inserting the tip under one of Christina's wings, he made only the slightest of motions, and the wing was torn clean away from her body, flying through the air to land in a bloody heap just a few feet from Billy.

"Never did like leg of chicken, anyway," laughed the farmer, almost drowned out by Christina's screaming. A waterfall of blood was pouring from her gaping, jagged stump, and it was obvious to Billy that she would die within minutes. But the farmer had not finished yet.

"You can help me test a little theory," he said, and with a single stroke of his knife, he lopped Christina's head clean off her body. Her jugular vein severed, blood jetted five or six feet into the air, and the farmer let it wash over his grimy face, cackling with sadistic delight. Then, very gingerly, he placed Christina's corpse onto the ground. But it didn't stay there.

Oh no! Like some grisly zombie, it was up and off, running around and around in circles, blood squirting and whirling in every direction, like a garden sprinkler from Hell. Finally, all reflexes ceased and poor, dead Christina tumbled into a heap, a perfect feast for the worms and vultures.

"*Come on out, the rest of you!*" *shrieked the farmer, advancing menacingly. "You'll never get away!"*

Poor Billy had never been so scared in his life, and he started to cry big, salty tears as the farmer seized Vernon the Vole and dragged him out of the undergrowth where he had been hiding. Instead of using the Bowie knife on Vernon, the farmer produced a red Swiss army penknife, and using one of the smaller, sharper blades, slit open Vernon's belly, as the little vole struggled and shrieked like Billy-o. Then he thrust his hand into the dying animal's cavity, and systematically began disembowelling him.

Out came Vernon's gizzard, all scarlet and sticky with blood. Then his stomach, still full of grass from last night's supper. And then his intestine, his oesophagus and his liver and spleen. The farmer made a whistling noise, and his wiry terrier dog, Tommy, raced up, and gobbled up the pile of bloodied and still piping-hot offal in an instant.

Bellowing with laughter, the farmer whirled Vernon's still-living body around his head, and tossed it away into the far distance.

The little dog laughed too, as Vernon's blood dribbled from his slavering jaws, and his pancreas, which had been too bitter to swallow, fell back into the dewy grass."

Norman Lewis smiled. "I told you there was a twist, Mr. Shandie. What do you think of it so far?"

"I feel sick," said Bob Shandie, who had turned a distinct shade of green. "I think that's enough,

Mr. Lewis. I don't want to hear any more."

"NO!" screamed the little man, rising to his feet and flailing his arms like a windmill. "This is the best bit! Let me finish! LET ME FINISH!"

When Shandie offered no further resistance, he sat back down and continued:

"What a to-do! Two of Billy's friends dead already, and the rest in mortal danger! Billy was too petrified to move, as the farmer leaned down to Tommy the dog and said something very quietly. Tommy nodded attentively, and then raced into a nearby copse at lightning speed. A few seconds later, he returned, with poor Myfanwy the Mole in his jaws. Did she struggle and scream, and utter strange Welsh curses, but the vicious little dog wouldn't let go.

There he sat, at the feet of his master, Myfanwy clamped between his savage incisors, and looked up for his next order. The farmer pondered for a moment, and then, with an evil leer, made a gesture of chewing food.

The dog understood instantly, and began to masticate. KER-RUNCH! went the jaws, as Myfanwy's pelvis shattered, and the little mole's screams reached ear-splitting proportions. A second later, Myfanwy exploded into a balloon of blood and guts as the dog's teeth tore apart her stomach. MUNCH! SCRUNCH! In a few seconds, only Myfanwy's head remained visible outside the jaws, her face set into a rictus death grimace bespeaking immeasurable agony. Then – with a slurp and a burp – even that was gone, and the doggie sat licking his lips, with a warm, full and contented tummy.

"And now for the ringleader," said the farmer grimly, brushing aside the foliage behind which Billy was hiding, and lifting him clean off his feet.

"Please, sir," wept Billy, "I'll pay you back for all the apples. Please don't kill me today."

"Certainly not," said the farmer with a broad grin, and for a moment Billy thought he was saved. Then his heart sank as the farmer continued, "As the ring-leader, you don't deserve a quick death. I'm going to make you suffer for hours and hours."

Then he brought out the little penknife that had so cruelly killed Vernon, and Billy strained and screamed, but it was all to no avail. Instead of the knife blade he had used before, the farmer this time brought out the corkscrew, which he inserted into Billy's little badger bottom, and twisted savagely until it had penetrated three inches in, tearing Billy's rectum clean away, and cruelly perforating his lower intestine.

Billy screamed pitifully, as his body was wracked with spasms of pain so intense he thought he must die. Instead, his agony continued as the farmer carried him back towards the farmhouse, dangling limply from the corkscrew blade on which he was irretrievably impaled.

"A good day's work, all told," said the farmer to his dog, in his attractive West Country burr. "They won't be stealing our apples again!"

The little dog laughed, then barked excitedly.

"What's that you say, Tommy? What are we going to do with this one?" The dog nodded frantically. "Oh

well, I thought we'd use him for our perverted sexual gratification throughout the night." The dog danced a cartwheel of delight. "Then in the morning, if he's still alive, we'll toss him into the combine harvester, and see how long he lasts."

And the happy dog giggled to see such fun as they strolled off home, leaving behind a trail of Billy's anal blood that was redder than a Russian spy embarrassed by being caught scoffing red peppers with tomato ketchup."

There was a very long pause, then Lewis said, "Well, Mr. Shandie, I think you'll agree it's certainly innovative. No-one's tried to fuse infants' television and the horror genre like this before."

Shandie, who had been sitting with his head in his hands, looked up with a new-found determination. "All right, you bloody loon, I'll humour you for five minutes, then out you go. Assuming this weren't the most disgusting, depraved, perverted piece of rubbish I've ever been subjected to, even in the unlikely event that any child watching it wouldn't suffer nightmares for weeks and probably irreparable personality damage, how in Christ's name do you propose to maintain the series when you've killed off all the principal characters?"

"Oh, that," said Lewis, unperturbed. "That's no problem. I'll just introduce another lot of animals in the next episode. In fact, I've done the synopsis already. The animals get caught in the middle of a motorway building project, and the workmen torture them with chainsaws and pickaxes before roasting them alive over their braziers."

"Right, that's it!" said Shandie. "Out! Out! And if you come within a mile of this office again, I'll get my security staff to give you a good kicking. Now bugger off back to Warminster, you sad psycho!"

And with that, he began manhandling the strange little fellow towards the door, who surprisingly did not struggle. *(The strange little fellow, that is, not the door. Not the most grammatical of sentences, I'll admit, but I really can't be bothered to go back and change it. Actually, maybe I should have had the door struggling. That would make a suitably surreal image.)*

"Oh, please," he was saying, "Please give me a job as a writer. That old house is so big and so lonely, with only mummy's mummified corpse for company. I need to get out more. I'll be good, I promise. You won't know I'm here at all. Look, I'll rework *The Animals Of Hampton Dell* any way you wish. I'll even take out the violent bits!"

Now they had reached the door. Norman Lewis tried one last gambit. "OK, OK, my script was rubbish. I admit it. I'll tear it up when I get outside. But please, please, let me be script editor for *Ali Butt And His Fishy Friends*. I love that show."

"Right," said Shandie, relaxing his grip. "This had better be good. What would you do if you were script editor of *Ali Butt*?"

"Well, I thought I'd have Pete the Pike torn to pieces in a piranha attack, Barbara the Brill slowly dying after being mutilated by a tungsten fishing-hook, Bernard the Gurnard being electrocuted by Ernie the Eel, who then hangs himself in a fit of remorse, and all the rest of the characters being caught by a Russian trawler and processed into fish fingers, which I'd show in graphic detail. That would leave Ali with his dogfish Rover as his only friend in the world – only Rover gets piscine distemper and has to be put down by the nurse shark, after which Ali pines slowly to death."

"*Ali Butt* is a programme for pre-school children, you moron," said Shandie through gritted teeth. "Children love Ali and his friends. They'd be absolutely devastated. Now FUCK OFF!"

And with that he delivered a hefty kick up Norman Lewis's posterior, and sent him sprawling into the corridor.

Chapter Three
C/U Fanny.

After he had ejected Lewis from his office, Bob Shandie settled down at his desk to collect his thoughts and calm himself down. After what seemed like five minutes, but was in fact far longer, he made for the door to welcome the next hopeful. It was only on checking his watch that he realised how late he was now running.

"Come in, come in!" he gestured to the man. "Look, I'm awfully sorry. We're ninety minutes late, which is appalling even by our standards. I can't apologise enough. I hope you haven't got far to go home."

"Not at all." It was a crisp, businesslike public school accent. "Ealing, old chap. Be there in a jiffy. No need to apologise about the delay."

Shandie settled himself down, and had his first good look at the man. The chap was probably in his mid-forties, slightly greying, and very smartly attired in what looked a Savile Row bespoke suit, heavy white silk shirt and red paisley cravat. He looked like a senior City broker or management consultant dressing down for the day, although Shandie had a suspicion he might actually be a professional scriptwriter. In any case, he seemed in an entirely different league to the morning's other hopefuls.

"Well, that's very kind of you," said Shandie, "Mr. … er…"

"Selkirk. Maurice Selkirk."

"Now, Mr. Selkirk, before we go any further, there are a couple of questions I must ask you, because I don't want to waste your time any more than you do."

"Quite, quite." The smart man seemed supremely confident and relaxed. "Ask away, sir, ask away."

"Now – your concept doesn't involve a woman with performing breasts, by any chance?"

Maurice Selkirk burst out laughing. "Afraid not, old boy, although I'd love to meet one. What an odd question."

"Yes, well… I met someone this morning who thought that would be a good way to appeal to fathers watching with their children."

"No, no, it's the mothers who usually watch with the kids, old chap," said Selkirk crisply. "Research proves that conclusively."

Shandie was impressed. "You've done your homework."

Maurice Selkirk tapped his nose. "Between you and me, old boy, research is my business. I'm an investigative journalist. Thought a bit of children's fiction might be a nice sideline, but don't tell my boss down at *The Times*."

This impressed Shandie even more. "You write for *The Times*?"

"Yes, old boy. Now what other preliminary questions did you want to ask me?"

"Does your proposed programme contain any scenes of graphic violence?"

"No, of course not. Even *Skydog And Webcat* is a bit aggressive for my tastes. Look, you seem a bit on edge, dear fellow. Is something the matter?"

Shandie shook his head wearily. "You'll have to forgive me. I've just met a couple of total weirdoes and they unnerved me a bit, that's all. You're the first normal person I've encountered all morning."

"Well, I do my best, old chap. I do my best."

"OK, then. Tell me about your concept."

Selkirk leaned forward conspiratorially. "Well, you know how children love playing Doctors and Nurses?"

Shandie leaped to his feet on a reflex. "No, I'm sorry, if you're suggesting we make a programme showing children looking at each others' bottoms and genitals, I must ask you to leave."

He was met by a gale of laughter. "You really *are* nervous, aren't you?" said Selkirk smoothly. "Relax. You're dealing with a professional now. This has nothing to do with looking at kiddies' arses. I only said it was *inspired* by Doctors and Nurses." Shandie sat down sheepishly, and Selkirk continued. "Now, if there's one programme my two youngest nippers love, it's *General Hospital*. You know the one?"

"The soap opera about a hospital, screened around 4pm?"

"Yes, that's the one. Catches them just as they get home from school. Well, my idea is to do a version of that with kids."

Bob Shandie sat back and pondered, ruminatively sucking on his rolled gold Parker pen. "Do you know, I quite like that. And that's the first time I've said that today. What do you propose – a format like *General Hospital* with a pool of characters, or one central character running throughout the show?"

"I would have thought one central character would be more interesting."

"I quite agree." Shandie nodded vigorously. "There's something in this. There's definitely something in this."

Maurice Selkirk looked pleased with himself. "Thought you'd say that, old boy. I've typed up a full shooting script for the first episode, as well. None of your handwritten scribblings here."

"I'll look forward to that. But first, I'm a little worried about the title. *Doctors And Nurses* could put a lot of parents off."

"I quite agree. That's why I propose we name it after our main character."

Excellent, thought Shandie, excellent! Things were looking up. The bloke had an intelligent idea, he seemed to understand the children's TV market, and his thinking was carefully considered. "Good man," he said. "And who is your central character?"

"Geoff The Gynaecologist," said Selkirk.

There was a stunned silence.

"Geoff is a *gynaecologist?*" said Bob Shandie.

"Yes, old boy. Is that a problem?"

"Well, yes, I think it might be. Couldn't we

have *Chris The Chiropodist* instead?"

Selkirk waved a warning finger. "Careful, old boy. Don't want people thinking we're a bunch of raving foot-fetishists. Anyway, gynaecology is a far more interesting discipline."

"Well, quite, but… I mean… you're not proposing we have Geoff examining semi-naked little girls, are you?"

Another laugh. "Of course not. That would be crazy." Shandie relaxed. "All his patients will be aged about sixteen or seventeen." Shandie tensed up again. "Look, see for yourself, old boy. Have a read of the script."

Shandie took the document with some trepidation, opened it at random and started to read. If nothing else, it was professionally laid out like a proper shooting script.

SCENE SEVEN

Geoff's consulting rooms. Daylight. Establishing shot of clock confirming 11:00 am. Tina (patient) walks in. She is aged about 17. Bobby socks, candy-pink mini-skirt, cropped top. Something of a Lolita.

Cut to: Geoff looking over his glasses.

GEOFF: Come in, Miss…

TINA: Samuels.

GEOFF: Samuels. Now, what seems to be the problem?

She sits down seductively, crossing her legs. C/U of legs.

TINA: I've got rather an embarrassing… discharge.

GEOFF   Don't be embarrassed. I'm a gynaecologist.

TINA: *(teasingly)* I can see that… big boy.

C/U of Geoff. He is somewhat ill-at-ease.

GEOFF   Er… can you describe this discharge?

TINA: Well, it's wet.

GEOFF   Yes.

TINA: That's all I can say, really.

GEOFF: Ah, well, that doesn't help me much. Would you like me to examine you on the couch?

TINA: *(giggling)* You saucy boy.

GEOFF: Ah… well… if you could go behind the screens, remove your underwear and lie down. I'll be in in a minute.

TINA: *I'll keep it warm for you.*

SCENE EIGHT

Behind the screen. Two or three minutes later. Tina is lying on the couch, naked from her waist to her knees. Her legs are spread wide apart and are up in stirrups. Geoff is adjusting an eyeglass.

TINA: *You know, I haven't been in this position since last Thursday.*

GEOFF: *Oh? You saw another gynaecologist then?*

TINA: *No, but it was one hell of a party.*

Geoff places the eyeglass in his eye.

GEOFF: *Right, let's have a look at you.*

C/U fanny.

Shandie almost dropped the script. "*C/U fanny?* You mean a close-up shot of a teenage girl's vulva?"

"Well, yes, old boy. That's what C/U normally means, doesn't it?"

"That's not what I meant. You can't show a teenage girl's pudendum on TV."

"Why not? It's been done before. If there's a legal problem, we can get an actress who's just turned eighteen… if we really need to."

"Good day, Mr. Selkirk." Shandie handed him

back his script. "I thought you were different from the others, but you're just as crazy as the rest."

"Don't agree with you," said Selkirk amiably, fetching his hat and coat. "You mark my words, *Geoff The Gynaecologist* will be on the box before the end of the year. You're missing out on a big opportunity."

"This is mad," said Shandie. "You said yourself that not many dads watch kids' TV, so who on earth is this show aimed at?"

Selkirk tapped his nose again, in the same infuriating manner. "Ah, that's the thing!" he chuckled. "Lesbian mums! Totally neglected up until now. Good day to you."

"Hang on, hang on!" Shandie called him back, perversely fascinated. "I think there's something a bit wrong with your logic. Lesbians don't tend to be mums. Do you know any lesbian mums?"

"My wife?"

"Your *wife* is a lesbian?"

Selkirk shook his head. "Well, she's in denial, put it that way. I keep telling her she should try it, and she says it doesn't appeal. Damn shame, really."

"Oh," said Shandie sarcastically. "My heart bleeds."

"Well, such is life. Might have more luck with my fifteen-year-old daughter. Now, *she* has some cute little chums. Pip, pip, old boy!"

As the door closed behind him, Bob Shandie sank into his chair, his eyes closed tight in agony. This was it, he concluded. No more Talent Days.

He would notify Kitty, his secretary, immediately, and they would stop placing the ads. All he had to do was work his way through the waiting list – which, unfortunately, meant about another six months of awful Thursdays.

If only, he thought, if only he had continued to pursue his very first career, as a publisher's reader. All you got were the manuscripts, not the nutters themselves, and if you didn't like them you could stop reading after five minutes and dictate a standard rejection letter. Furthermore, you found a better class of person writing novels than kids' TV. A lot of the stuff was awful, but rarely was it offensive. Finding something simultaneously awful, offensive and also a bit scary, like the stuff he had been presented with, was very, *very* unusual indeed – to say the least.

Part Five: God.

Chapter One
Virgins Off The Starboard Bow.

"**F**or fuck's sake, son!" screamed God, banging on the bathroom door with his beefy fist. "Will you hurry it up, you little twat?"

A muffled reply came through the cheap, white-painted plywood. "'n' 'v'n' a 'it."

"Oh, come on!" God was now slamming his head against the door in frustration, albeit lightly. "I've got to be at work by nine! If I'm late again, that sanctimonious bloody archangel Gabriel will never let me hear the end of it."

The only response was the muffled, though quite distinct, sound of a toilet flushing. After a few seconds' hesitation, the door opened a crack, and Jesus's bearded face appeared around it.

"Hold your horses, Dad. Can't a bloke even have a shit in peace these days?"

He need not have bothered to explain what he had been doing: the noxious aroma of last night's vindaloo, defecated in as liquid a form as it had been consumed, was wafting through the door, and for a moment seemed capable of engulfing the whole of Heaven.

"Fuckin' Jesus!" God clasped a hand to his outraged nose. "What the fuck have you got up your arse? A dead fucking animal?"

"Just had a bit of a night out with the lads, that's all. A few pints down the Pangolin And Sampling Synthesiser…"

"About fifteen, if I know your mates," said God.

"Then on to the Star of Bengal for a vindaloo or three. I must say, that one was a bit of a ring-stinger."

"Nose stinger, an' all," said God. "I've got to have my morning bath in the middle of that – should have brought a fucking gas mask."

"Wrong," said Jesus. "What we need is a second bathroom. I've been telling you that for years."

God shook his head sadly. "You just don't listen, do you? We – can't – fucking – afford it. I'm up to my overdraft limit as it is. That poxy builder who created the universe went way over estimate – BASTARD!"

"Come on mate, you're the supreme being of the universe. You created Heaven and Earth, and everything in it. Financing a second bathroom shouldn't be beyond your abilities."

"I've tried, son, I've tried. Even went down the bank to see old Bloodstone, ask whether he'd mind letting us have a little advance."

"And?"

"Said if I asked again, it'd take a ten-foot bargepole to remove his presentation Bugatti desk pen set from my arsehole."

Jesus laughed. "Now I know why we stay with that bank. It's because they give us service with a smile."

"No, it's because nobody else would have us,

the state our account's in. Now get your arse out of that bathroom, it's twenty-five past eight."

"Won't be five minutes – I've just got to shave." And with that, the bathroom door slammed shut again.

For a moment God pondered this latest utterance, then realisation dawned. "You lying twat, you've got a beard! You're just trying to make me late." And with that, he recommenced his angry battery on the long-suffering yet hard-wearing door until, without warning, the wood splintered and his fist went right the way through.

As God withdrew his hand, Jesus's face appeared through the jagged hole, grinning from ear to ear. "That'll cost you, mate!"

"That's what you think, pal," replied God, with more than a hint of pride. "I've planned ahead on this one. Our household insurance now includes accidental damage."

"Yeah, I know that. But I think if you check the small print, you'll find that Acts of God are specifically excluded. So let's hope you can up the overdraft after all."

By lunchtime, God's mood had lightened somewhat: at least, as much as is possible for a man with the largest overdraft in the known universe. Indeed, his expression had taken on something of a religious countenance, and unusually he was not swearing much. This was normally a sign he had done something wrong and was trying to wriggle out of it.

"Son," he said quietly. "You and I need a serious discussion. Would you mind asking those angels to leave us for some minutes?"

Jesus nodded. "Sure, Dad. FUCK OFF YOU WINGED WANKERS!"

The angels dispersed immediately, and God winced. "Now I know why I made you Personnel Director round here. You have such a way with the staff."

"Don't even know why we employ the fuckers. Sitting on clouds, wearing white dresses – even the blokes, the great nancies – and strumming harps. Lazy toerags! Wouldn't be so bad if they played a decent instrument like the electric guitar – nice Hendrix riff or two."

"Unfortunately," said God, "Rock and roll is the Devil's music."

"Yes, and it's totally wasted on that mincing old queen. Only thing he likes is show tunes."

"He's recently developed a liking for boy bands," said God, then after a pause, "He's quite fond of their music, as well. Anyway, sit yourself down, son, time you and I had a man-to-man chat."

"Oh God," said Jesus, flopping down into a voluminous but tatty green armchair. "You're not going to ask to borrow my porn stash again, are you? Because the answer's no, after the state they came back in last time. Couldn't open any of the fucking pages."

God grinned self-indulgently. "Oh no, son. Won't be needing that. Don't need that at all."

Jesus was immediately suspicious. "And what does that mean, you old fucker?"

God's expression became even more sanctimonious, if that were possible. "Verily," he said, "It was written of old that God did love the world so much, he sent his only son for to be crucified for their sins. And lo, didst he suffer on that fated Hill of Golgotha."

When God spoke in a biblical manner, it was always a sign that something extremely bad was coming. Jesus prepared himself for the worst.

"And yea, even his glorious death did not absolve sin from the hearts of men. And so, two thousand years hence, God didst look down upon the sins of the world in great sorrow, and he did decide that the time was right for the Second Coming of his beloved…"

Jesus leapt to his feet, shouting. "What? Have I heard you right, you old twat? You've got some fucking bird up the duff again?"

God cowered, as Jesus actually seemed angry enough to punch him. "Well, life's been hell since your mum left me for that arsehole Judas Iscariot. I've been wanking so much I've got a right arm like Popeye. Come on, come on, I'm the celestial ruler of the universe – I'm entitled to the odd shag."

"Haven't you ever heard of contraception, you dozy cunt? But oh no, that'd be too much trouble for you, you lazy pillock. It just amazes me that any woman would want to fuck a grizzled old goat like you."

"Come on son, you've got to admit that 'I am the deity incarnate, and our child will be the new Messiah' is quite a chat-up line."

Jesus snorted. "So is 'I've got a ten-inch knob and you can sit on it till it turns blue', but that doesn't mean any intelligent bird will fall for it. So who is this woman? Anything like my last mother on earth?"

God smiled wistfully. "Ah yes, Mary. Doesn't seem 2000 years ago, does it? What a wonderful, sweet, innocent girl. So perfect a subject for the Virgin Birth."

"Virgin? That scabby old tart had more pricks up her than a pin cushion. Joseph said fucking her was like throwing a sausage up the Mersey Tunnel."

"No, no, that's a scurrilous lie. She is revered by the True Church as the source of all purity and chastity."

Jesus laughed. "That's thanks to a bloody translation error. Amazing that the Old Sanskrit for 'celestial virgin' is so similar to 'fucking old slapper'. Imagine how the Catholic church would have turned out if they'd read it properly – you'd have convent girls fucking everything in sight and giving blowjobs left, right and centre."

Now God's grin spread from ear to ear. "The ones I know do, mate, no sweat."

"Oi." Jesus wagged an accusing finger. "The mother superior banned you from that convent school. Said if you went back and molested any more of her girls, she'd cut your balls off with a penknife."

"Pity. Best days of my life."

Jesus had not finished with his discourse on his first earthly mother. "And another thing about Mary. She really was a kinky bitch…"

"Well," said God, with a mischievous grin, "She did like taking it up the shitter."

"Pity you didn't fuck her there more often. I wouldn't have had to have gone down at all."

"Yes, going down, she liked that as well," said God. "And she always swallowed."

"Well, you nearly swallowed Joseph's fist when he found out. How on earth did you explain you were fucking his fiancée?"

"Well, we came to an arrangement."

"What sort of arrangement?"

"Put it this way. That's one of the reasons why the overdraft is so high, and we can't afford a second bathroom."

The fight largely gone out of him, Jesus fell back down into the armchair, his face in his hands. "For fuck's sake, Dad, I can't go back there. Those people are psychos. They nailed me to a fucking tree last time – and a fat lot of use you were!"

"Come on son, won't be so bad. You'll meet lots of nice new girls to shag, and they've got plenty of good pubs and curry houses. Also, they've got a lot more civilised over the last two millennia. You should be OK."

"Well, thank you Mr. Talking-Brochure-For-The-Planet-Earth, but I've still got to go through the childhood thing. Lying about, wearing those shitty nappies…"

"Lots of blokes would pay good money for that," interjected God.

"And getting spanked whenever I'm naughty…"

"Ditto."

"And having to go to school for 12 years."

"Ah yes, but think of all the schoolgirls."

"What, the five or six-year-olds? What do you think I am, a fucking nonce?"

God sighed. "Let's not bicker, son. It's too late, anyway. I did my best to have you aborted, but she was having none of it. In eighteen weeks, you'll be born, and there's nothing either of us can do about it."

"Give me her address and a rusty coathanger, and I'll have a bloody good try."

"No, son, it's no use. You'll just have to make the best of it."

Jesus was still in a towering fury, but beginning to accept the idea. "Well, OK, but I'm not doing any of that preaching and miracles nonsense that got me into trouble last time."

"Bollocks. You're a natural show-off. You'll be walking on water every day to persuade some tart to drop her knickers."

(Author's note: I nearly typed "drop her knockers" there instead, which was definitely a Freudian slip, but the wonders of the modern word-processor enabled me to cover my embarrassment – or it would have done, if I hadn't decided to include this Author's note. Although it doesn't make much sense, I think her "dropping her knockers" is rather

*an interesting image, and I get the impression that
Jesus probably agrees with me.)*

"So what's my new family like, then?" said Jesus.
"Hopefully very rich, with a stately home, a few
hundred acres of land, plenty of servants, and a
few cute sisters for me to have a bit of incestuous
fun with."

"Wrong on the last bit," said God, "you'll be
an only child. Wrong on all of it, in fact. Your
mother-to-be is a delightful young lady, however."

"Not the usual sort of ropy old hag you go for,
then?"

"No, no, she is a lady of delicacy and refinement."

"Cut the crap, and tell me her name and where
she comes from."

God realised the game was up. "Her name
is Michelle, and she lives on a council estate in
Basildon."

Jesus's eyebrow arched. "Oh, yes. Classy bird,
then is she?"

Chapter Two
Three-Headed Dog.

For those souls who had recently died and ascended to Heaven, the Pearly Gates must have come as an impressive – as well as a welcome – sight. Fifteen feet high at their peak, opalescent and gem-encrusted, they had been finely wrought in an elegant neoclassical design that somehow reminded one of the miniature harps carried by beatific angels, and also embodied some of the gossamer delicacy of the selfsame angels' wings.

Yet these apparently innocuous gates also contained surprising strength. When locked, they would have been impossible to force open, even were it not for the 400,000 volt charge passed through them to deter intruders. That a warm welcome might not await all was further reinforced by the notice "Beware of the Bouncer" prepared by a humorous angel, and attached to the gates at eye level.

It was not an inappropriate sentiment, as could be confirmed by one's first glimpse of St. Peter. Six feet four in height and seventeen-and-a-half-stone, he resembled nothing so much as a grim-faced gorilla that had been partially shaved and then clad in an ill-fitting dinner suit for a chimps' tea party.

The shiny black suit, of an unmistakable 1970s cut, was offset by a frilly wing-collared shirt and a huge, floppy black bow tie, and surmounted by Peter's grim face, with its unblinking gimlet eyes and sinister square-cut black goatee. During his life, Peter had been a debt collector by day for the long-established Galilee firm of Cohen & Sons *("instant shekels with a smile, late repayments with a broken kneecap")*, for whom he had administered savage beatings to many impoverished members of the local community.

(Mediaeval scholars, wishing to raise his status somewhat, had deliberately mistranslated his rôle as "tax collector", which conjures up genteel images of a suited gentleman calculating liabilities with an abacus, and politely threatening violence via buff OHMS envelopes. Then, to cover their tracks further, they transferred his profession to fellow disciple Matthew, and claimed he had been a fisherman.)

By night, he had doubled his income as Chief Doorman for the seediest nightspot in Nazareth, the Pharisee-À-Go-Go, where his fearsome reputation had spread far and wide. Jesus had been something of a regular at the club, since it maintained a relaxed door policy towards under-clad underage girls, and had been one of the few people to make friends with the ill-tempered bouncer.

Indeed, that temper was now being vented on a harmless middle-aged man, who looked like a mid-ranking cost accountant, who was standing, panting *(as well he might, after 12,436 steps)* at the top of the pearly staircase. As God and Jesus approached from inside the gates, an argument was in full swing.

"No, you are not on the fucking guest list," bellowed Peter at the cowering recently deceased. "And if you're not on the list, you don't fucking come in."

"But I've been a God-fearing man all my life," ventured the accountant. "There must be some sort of mistake. I can't be down for Hell. Couldn't you check with your Guv'nor or something?"

This enraged Peter even more. "Look sonny, I fucking decide who comes in here and who doesn't, not the fucking management. Even if I took pity on you, you couldn't come in because of the dress code."

The man looked flummoxed. "What dress code?"

"It's perfectly clear, you twat. You should have read it before you started up the stairs. No blue jeans!"

The accountant looked down at his smartly pressed Levi's, then attempted to salvage the situation with a little wit. "Why, what colour jeans would I need to wear to get in?"

"You cheeky cunt!" screamed Peter, leaping forward and headbutting the man viciously. The bloke tumbled backwards, clutching his nose, and rolled down a dozen or so steps before coming to rest, leaving a river of blood behind him. "Now fuck off downstairs where you belong, or prepare to die for a second time!"

The accountant crawled off down the stairs, still clutching his injured proboscis. God and Jesus clapped derisorily.

"Thanks lads," said St. Peter.

"Nice one, mate," said Jesus. "He looked a boring bastard anyway. Probably would have applied to become an angel."

Peter grunted. "So what brings you out here, boss? Going down to Earth again to see your lady friend?"

"Quite the reverse." God gestured downwards with his thumb.

"Fuck," said Peter. "You're visiting 'er majesty."

"Yes. It's to do with Jesus's impending birth. I wanted to ask for his co-operation. You know, make sure he doesn't go down to Earth…"

"Up," said St. Peter.

"… up to Earth and start tempting him again."

"Oh no, that Devil's quite a little tease," said Peter thoughtfully. "Well, mind you've put on reinforced underpants, that's all I say."

"And slip-on shoes," ventured Jesus with a snigger.

God rounded on him. "One more crack and you'll be coming with me."

"One more crack…" chortled Peter. "How very appropriate."

Jesus shook his head with a grin. "Oh no, mate. You started all this by fucking that girl without a johnny. You get down there and sort it out, and I hope he fucks your arse off."

"Pillock," retorted God, and started down the stairs, in search of the express elevator.

Several million miles below, Hell was, as ever, pleasantly warm, and its usual rich, throbbing red colour. Indeed, the place resembled the inside of an artery, or perhaps some trendy nightspot, where the lighting was kept permanently low to disguise the fact that the women in the skimpy dresses were all in their forties, leaving their drunken paramours to experience the full horror of realisation on waking up next to them the following morning.

Generally it was a friendly place – although anyone male and under about 40 was well advised to keep a close eye on his bottom – but today the Devil seemed in a particularly bad mood. The horned leather head-dress atop his hairy head was quivering with fury, his eyes had taken on a maniacal glint, and his petite frame – clad in a giant leather codpiece, thigh boots, and a sort of odd bondage arrangement around the upper torso that left his hairy chest clearly on view – seemed uncharacteristically large and threatening.

The object of his wrath was a nervous-looking fellow in a business suit, who was straining to hold on to a particularly vicious three-headed dog. This was Cerberus, the famed Hound of Hell, which had come part and parcel with the fixtures and fittings when the Devil had purchased Hell from its previous owner, Hades.

In fact, the inclusion of the dog at no extra charge had been the only concession the Greek God had been prepared to offer. Other than that, he had been a total pain, wrangling for weeks over the price, constantly changing the completion date, and generally running the estate agent, Mr. Brendon Pierce of Oxtaby Dennison & Mallahide, ragged. Pierce had openly confessed to the Devil that he hated dealing with archaic foreign deities, as they were always opinionated nuisances. The Roman and Greek Gods were the worst, however, because of their unstable Latin temperaments.

Finally, the deal had been agreed, with the dog included at no charge. In fact, now that the Devil thought back, Hades had offered a discount for taking the dog – as well as making it a condition of the sale. Now he knew why the slippery Greek had been so keen to leave the animal behind.

"So," he addressed the businessman. "Let's get this straight, ducky. I bought the nicest piece of fillet steak in the shop for my supper, thinking I'd have it with a glass or two of Côtes du Rhône, and you've fed it to the dog."

"Yes, sir," stammered the businessman. "You see, he was very hungry, and as his h-handler…"

The man was indeed Cerberus's personal handler, a rôle traditionally reserved for the most evil sinner in Hell. It was always difficult for the Devil to decide on the most suitable appointee, and usually he restricted the post to someone who had inflicted untold suffering on millions of innocent human beings. The current postholder fitted the bill perfectly, as he had been instrumental in discovering the Spice Girls.

"He was hungry?" shrieked the Devil. "So you fed my beautiful fillet steak to that mangy, flea-ridden old…"

Seemingly able to understand the conversation, the dog was becoming agitated. Low, menacing growls were emitting from all three of its throats, flabby wet black lips drawn back from rows of razor sharp canine teeth. Its six hate-filled eyes were fixed like gimlets on its owner, and it was now straining so hard on its leash that the businessman's arms were beginning to slip from their sockets.

The Devil was well aware of the savage bites the animal could inflict, and quickly reversed his tack. "Oh well, that's fine then. I'm sure I've got some dry chicken at the back of the fridge that will do in a sandwich. After all," his voice took on the patronising singsong quality that people adopt when talking to children and animals, "only the best will do for my lovely Cerby-Werby."

With that, he reached out and stroked the nearest head. The dog responded by snapping at his fingers, and only narrowly missed.

An awkward silence followed, broken when a messenger arrived and tapped the devil on the shoulder.

"Ooh!" said the Devil. "Is that a note in your pocket, or are you just pleased to see me?"

"No, it's a note. Your old Guv'nor's just arrived to see you."

"He is not my old Guv'nor! I left that hairy homophobe's firm as soon as I could get away. Yes, that's just what I need – the dog's eaten my supper, and now I've got to contend with the Beer Monster."

With that, he turned and raced furiously away down the corridor, only too aware that the Supreme Manifestation of Evil's work is never done.

God was waiting just outside the lift, looking resplendent – but very out of place – in his flowing white robes. The Devil took several minutes to reach him, having stopped off at his apartment to change into a clean ceremonial codpiece. Now he advanced on God, grinning, his hand outstretched in welcome. God shook it warily.

"So, how are you keeping, lovey? Don't see you down here much."

"No, no, lots to do, you know." The two men were habitually awkward with one another. "Just thought I'd drop by for a…" Small-talk was not God's forté. He was loath to go straight into his request, as the Devil might be more co-operative if he couched his mission as a social visit. Struggling for something to say, he added, "How's that lovely dog of yours?"

"Oh, fine, fine."

"Wish we had something like that in Heaven, to keep out the riff-raff."

"Who needs a three-headed dog when you've got St. Peter?" A feverishly evil idea suddenly occurred to the Devil. "Tell you what, why don't we swap?"

God laughed. "I don't think so, mate. Doesn't your dog just piss and shit all over the place, anywhere it likes?"

"Well, yes. But so does St. Peter."

God nodded. "True, true. One thing I've been meaning to ask you…" God was genuinely interested in this issue. "Your dog has three mouths. Does he also have three arseholes?"

The Devil shook his head. "No, just the one arse. Produces enough shit for three dogs, though. I've got two blokes with shovels who do nothing but clean up behind him. Anyway," the Devil placed a hand on God's arm conspiratorially, "I didn't know you were so interested in arseholes."

God jumped like a scalded cat. Oh Christ, the conversation had got into dangerous waters. He had sudden visions of crawling back up to Heaven with a ringpiece like a doughnut, Jesus and Peter waiting at the Pearly Gates and pissing themselves laughing when they learned of his ordeal. Keeping his back pressed very firmly against the lift doors, he fumbled behind him for the button.

"Only joking, ducky! You're not my type at all. Whereas, that charming son of yours…"

"Ah, yes. It was Jesus I was wanting to talk to you about, anyway."

The Devil raised an eyebrow. "On the turn, is he? I always said heterosexuality was just a phase he was going through."

"Well, in that case he's been going through it for seven thousand years, since the day he was born. Your chances of shagging him are about the same as England winning Wimbledon."

"Well, they will, in five years' time," retorted the Devil. "Virginia Wade, in the women's singles." And then, as an aside to the reader, "Ooh, my psychic powers are sharp today. I'd better watch I don't scratch myself."

"That reminds me why I don't come to see you more often. You and your fucking occult predictions. It's always the same – if there's a good Agatha Christie on the box, you tell me the ending. If it's the World Cup, you ring me up with the result five minutes before the match starts."

"Silly game – 22 men kicking a pig's bladder around a field. Still, worth watching for their muscular hairy legs." The Devil slapped his own wrist. "What a naughty boy! Anyway, I didn't tell you the result last time a match was on."

"No – you just said not to bother watching because I wouldn't see any goals."

The Devil delivered another aside to the reader. "It annoys him greatly, methinks. Egad, I am a bounder."

God took a menacing step forward. "And stop talking to the reader," he bellowed, "this isn't a fucking Restoration comedy, you know."

"Verily, he hast tumbled my little game."

"I said SHUT IT! Now, back to Jesus. Having seen the continued sin of the world, I have decided with infinite regret to offer my only son once again as a sacrifice."

The Devil's eyes widened with amusement.

"You've shagged another slapper, haven't you? Go on, then – what's the dirty bitch's name?"

"I resent that allegation," said God haughtily. "I have very exacting standards in women."

"Yes: they've got to fuck on a first date, and swallow every time they give you a blowjob."

"Well, yes but…"

"I mean, remember that old tart Mary. She's one of the worst behaved residents we have here. Actually made a pass at me once. Got her tits out and everything."

"Wasted on you, you old poof," God muttered under his breath.

"What was that, ducky?" said the Devil menacingly. "And what exactly has Jesus being born again got to do with me?"

God was deeply embarrassed. Asking a favour from a former employee struck him as extremely humiliating: especially an employee who had set up a very successful firm of his own. "Well, er… I remember how badly you behaved the last time he was down there. I don't want you going up there and tempting him again."

"Sorry, dear. I'm just a little minx who can't help herself. Now then, are you getting back in the lift, or do I have to set the dog on you?"

God stepped backwards into the lift with an expression of fury on his face. "Mincing old queen," he muttered, as the doors closed.

"And give my love to St. Peter." The Devil blew him a kiss. "You tell that big, butch boy that if ever he wants someone to make a man of him, he knows where to come." The lift ascended out of sight, and with a girlish giggle he turned and stalked back into the heart of his kingdom.

Chapter Three
Beef Curtains With Tea.

Billy Bottomley, Chief Reader to Mackenzie & Dover, Publisher of Quality Novels, threw down the manuscript with disgust. The book was unbelievable: crude, blasphemous and painfully unfunny. Even the title *The Second Coming* – scrawled in marker pen across the cover of the typescript – was laden with the most witless form of innuendo.

Astonishing, he fulminated, astonishing that anyone could write such a thing, let alone send it to a publisher with the expectation that it might be accepted. Of course, one got to see a lot of dross these days, even through reputable agents, but this particular piece of crap marked a new low in his career. He began to sweat as he imagined the consequences of publishing such a work – the outrage from the Christian community, attempts to have the firm prosecuted for blasphemy, very likely protests from fundamentalists at his office. It would be like a Christian answer to *The Satanic Verses*, only sixteen years before the original was published!

Yet the book had a strange, grotesque fascination. It was almost impossible not to read on and find out what happened in this bizarre tale. In the meantime, however, what was required was a good cup of tea – not the easiest thing to find in the middle of France.

Apart from that, he could hardly fault his creature comforts. The Château de Porc-Sourde was one of the finest country houses in France, tastefully converted to a luxury hotel with space for just thirty guests. The lounge in which he was relaxing was opulence personified, with its high vaulted ceilings, rich burgundy walls, antique furniture, overstuffed armchairs and priceless tapestries. That was before one even considered the magnificence of the bedrooms, with their marvellous four-posters, large sitting areas, private balconies and pristine black-and-white Victorian bathrooms. Or the culinary and architectural splendour of the Roupettes-Sur-La-Langue restaurant, which held two Michelin stars, and was justifiably renowned as one of the finest eating places in Europe. Then there was the forty-five acres of verdant private grounds... Magnificent, he reflected, truly magnificent, and the one place where he was really able to concentrate on considering new works, undistracted by the hustle and bustle of the city.

Bottomley rose to his feet, stepping gingerly over the pile of manuscripts he had brought with him, and rang the bell for the servant. The only bad thing about the place, he concluded, was the terrible journey to get there.

The flight from Heathrow to Charles de Gaulle was simple enough, but there the fun and games began. First the TGV (Train à Grande Vitesse) to Rouen, then the TPV (Train à Petite Vitesse) from Rouen to Orly, then the TNV (Train à Non-Vitesse) from Orly to Rideaux-de-Boeuf via Lyon, Marseille, Strasbourg, Calais and Rennes-Le-Château, from where it was a half hour taxi ride to the Château itself. One was always positively exhausted on arrival, but the Comte de Porc-Sourde could be relied upon to provide a splendid personal service that cheered the spirit.

Just as Bottomley was settling himself down again, and adjusting his gold-rimmed spectacles, the day's duty waiter, Henri-Gaston Le Fauteuil-Confortable, arrived.

"*Oui, monsieur?*"

"A cup of tea, if you'd be so kind."

"*Certainement, monsieur.*" The waiter left the room discreetly. Bottomley was slightly surprised. Even as a regular VIP guest, one could not be sure of getting tea. The mere act of asking for it seemed to affront the sensibilities of the French, who thought one should be taking bitter jet-black coffee or perhaps a ludicrously overpriced cognac.

His worst fears were realised, as he heard an argument beginning to develop outside the door, just as he was picking up the blasphemous manuscript to continue reading.

The voices were inevitably muffled, but it sounded somewhat like Alain-Jean-Christophe C'est-Comme-Ça-Que-La-Roue-Tourne, the deputy duty manager. "*Une tasse de thé?*" he was saying.

"Mais ce n'est pas possible, ça! C'est onze heures du matin! Tu tire ma jambe, mon fils? Tu pense que je sois né hier? Tire l'autre, elle a les clôches attachées!"

At this rate, he thought, the argument could last for hours, and would end up involving David-François-Pierre-Paul Je-Me-Suis-Reveillé-Ce-Matin, the executive head chef, and Régis-Cyrille-Richard-Yves-Simon Les-Collines-Sont-Vivantes-Avec-Le-Son-De-La-Musique, the supervising hotel manager.

(It could also involve a lot of other French gentlemen with ridiculous and unfunny compound names if I were the sort of unscrupulous bastard who includes this kind of shit simply to boost the word count and take more money off you, but thankfully I'm not. Well, only a little anyway.)

Bottomley did not hear Henri-Gaston Le Fauteuil-Confortable's *(another five words used up there – and another six words in telling you that five words were used up there – and another fourteen words in telling you…)* reply to Alain-Jean-Christophe C'est-Comme-Ça-Que-La-Roue-Tourne, but finally Alain-Jean-Christophe C'est-Cómme-Ça-Que-La-Roue-Tourne conceded, *"Ah, c'est pour Monsieur* Bottomley! *Monsieur* Guillaume *Bottomley! Pas de problème, donc!"*

Bottomley sat back in satisfaction, and started to read again. Everything was all right. He was going to get his tea.

Chapter Four
Demons At Dawn.

The book did not become any less offensive as one read on. Jesus's second birth (or third, if you count the one in Heaven) was described in the most harrowing gynaecological detail – with copious mention of "excessive bleeding", "agonised screams" and "six stitches required to repair the gaping gash in her groin caused by the sudden appearance of the eleven-pound Saviour".

Bottomley winced, and, almost involuntarily, crossed his legs. He was still feeling queasy when his tea arrived, accompanied by a complimentary *(and also complementary)* selection of fine pâtisserie. Sipping his tea, he persevered with the book.

The section on Jesus's infancy was innocuous enough, but once he began school the book returned to form. One particular scene – which described a "steamy session" between a six-year-old Jesus and a classmate named Sharon – was clearly an incitement to paedophilia, and Bottomley lost patience with the offensive work. Flipping ahead a few pages, he found that the now-teenage Jesus was a prodigious womaniser and a regular user of hard drugs, not to mention leader of a vicious and destructive gang, "The Basildon Bastards", that held the local estate in a reign of terror.

Reasoning that he would give the book one final chance, Bottomley flipped ahead to the eleventh chapter, and read it in its entirety:

Chapter Eleven
The Not-Very-Final Temptation Of Christ (And It Wasn't That Tempting Anyway).

The scene for the Devil's renewed temptation of Christ could hardly compare to the barren Sinaï Desert in terms of spectacle. Indeed, the shabby parade of shops on the outskirts of Basildon made Third World slums look inviting by comparison. The Du Poppin Restaurant was set between a firm of pawnbrokers, their shopfront protected against vandals by a fine wire mesh grille, and a boarded-up hulk of a shop that had once sold scooters.

The café itself was even grubbier than its surroundings, grime smeared up the cracked plate glass window, and dirt caked into every crevice of the panelled front door. The Devil, dressed as always in his full diabolic regalia, regarded it with open revulsion. He did not like the world at the best of times – mainly because it was full of homophobes – and was also something of a gourmet. The thought of consuming even a cup of tea in such an unhygienic hovel made his stomach turn, but he was quite prepared to do so in the line of duty. After all, tempting people into sin was a serious business. It was not to be taken lightly.

The Devil had with him Cerberus, who as usual was slavering and growling and farting. In a surprising display of courage, the dog's handler had point blank refused to mind him for the day, and so the Devil had had no choice but to bring the repulsive animal with him on his little "field trip". Unlike his master, the dog seemed very excited by the Du Poppin – tempted, no doubt, by the stale smell of last week's fried sausages – and made a bolt for the door, dragging Satan in its wake.

"No!" Satan admonished him, hauling back on the lead. "Look – there's a sign on the door. It says 'No dogs. Especially three-headed ones.'"

The dog snarled and sulked as the Devil tied it up outside, and snapped at his heels as he wandered into the filthy café.

Jesus was already present, sitting at a nearby table and nursing a tea. Unusually, he had changed into full Biblical costume, complete with flowing hair, beard, white robe and sandals. The Devil concluded that he looked quite ridiculous, conveniently ignoring the fact that his own studded leather codpiece, bare chest and head-dress were attracting very odd looks from the waitress.

"Morning, ducks," said the Devil, sitting down.

"Hello, mate," said Jesus. "Good journey?"

"Well," said the Devil, "things are a lot quicker since Charon's bought that hovercraft. Crossing the Styx is three times as fast as with the old car ferry. Of course, it's also three times the price. A lot of the recently dead just leave their cars behind on the bank because they can't afford to bring them, so I never need to hire one."

Jesus nodded, uninterested. "Not a bad place, this, wouldn't you say?"

The Devil ran a cautious finger along the Formica table top. It was slick with grease.

"Well, it's not exactly the Café Royal, put it that way, but it's certainly your kind of gaff. I'm surprised you didn't choose a curry house."

Jesus shrugged. "On Earth, they don't open until lunchtime. In Heaven, they're open 24 hours a day, because that's the law."

Breaking the awkward moment, the waitress wandered over. Although only in her very early twenties, she looked much older, with her swept-back peroxide hair, clumsily applied and excessive make-up, and tight but dowdy brown-and-white uniform. The Devil thought she looked a frightful tart, but Jesus was regarding her ample bosom with evident interest.

"So what's it to be, lads?" she said, in a piercing Estuary English bray.

The Devil was about to ask whether there was any chance of a mixed leaf salad with walnut oil dressing, when Jesus interjected. "Two full English breakfasts, please, with extra bread-and-butter."

"Coming right up. Good party was it, boys?"

The Devil fixed her with a piercing stare. "What?"

"The fancy dress party you both went to last night. Must have been pretty good if you haven't had time to change."

"Yes," said Jesus. "Bloody good. I'll invite you

to the next one."

"Thanks, lover." The sluttish woman waggled her backside as she flounced off into the kitchen.

"And what did you say that for?" hissed the Devil. "I was about to tell the cheeky slag to mind her own business, and that she wasn't exactly the height of fashion herself."

"Yes, and then she'd have been wearing your bollocks as earrings." Jesus shook his head. "This is the East End, mate, not Hell. Nobody's afraid of you around here. In fact, I think you took a pretty big risk coming here dressed like that."

"Yes," said Satan drily. "I could say the same of you."

Jesus slurped his tea. "OK, let's get down to business. I've been on this poxy planet seventeen years, and this is the first time you've come to see me. What do you want?"

The Devil fluttered his eyelashes. "I've come to tempt you, my dear."

"What, like you tempted me last time? I'm sorry, but throwing myself off a cliff wasn't all that tempting."

"Oh, no. I wondered if I could tempt you with my bottom."

"No."

"Oh, go on."

"No."

"Please."

"No."

"You know you want to."

"No, I don't."

"You do really."

"No. I'm not gay."

"You are really."

"I'm not. I've been straight since I was born, seven thousand years ago."

"It's just a phase you're going through."

"No it isn't. I've got a girlfriend called Mandy."

"Bet her arse isn't as good as mine."

"Her arse is mindblowing. So's her fanny, which is tighter than a gnat's chuff. And her tits are fucking excellent as well."

"OK, then. Do it to make an old Devil very happy."

"Fuck off. If you want something up your bottom, use the sausage from your breakfast."

There was a lengthy silence, broken only when the Devil said, "You're no bloody fun. You never give in to temptation."

"Unless it comes from a 15-year-old with a 36DD chest," said Jesus longingly, and their breakfasts arrived shortly after.

The two men ate their food mainly in silence, Jesus enthusiastically gobbling his, whilst the Devil picked at his nervously and reluctantly. Finally, they finished, and were sipping the last of their tea and chatting desultorily, when the door flew open, and an angry-looking man clad in a blue serge uniform strode over to them.

"Is that your dog?" he demanded aggressively, wielding a notebook.

"Er, yes," said the Devil. "Is there a problem?

He hasn't bitten anyone, has he?"

"No, he hasn't bitten." The man fixed the Devil with a look of withering contempt. "He's just gone and shat all over the bloody pavement."

"Oh, he always does that."

"Not in fucking Basildon, he doesn't, sonny. We have very firm rules about that sort of thing. People who let their dogs shit on the pavement are subject to a mandatory £20 fine."

"Fuck," said the Devil.

"Only in your case, I'm going to make an exception."

"You mean, let me off because it's a first offence?"

"No, I mean fine you £60 because your dog's shit is three times the size of a normal dogshit. You can pay up immediately, then scrape up the fucker when you get outside."

"Fuckin' bastard," muttered the Devil, handing over six crisp tenners.

"I heard that," said the council official. He looked Jesus and the Devil up and down one last time. "Pair of poofs," he snorted, stalking back out of the café.

Jesus and the Devil sat staring at one another in silent fury.

By the time the Devil got outside, he was absolutely seething with rage. Anger, it seemed, had made him lose fear with the savage dog, which sat with a huge grin over all three of its faces, a mountain of dung more befitting of a baby elephant behind it.

"Right, you fucker," snarled the Devil. "You've

cost me sixty bloody quid this morning. So now I'm going to housetrain you, once and for all."

Jesus watched on, dumbfounded, as the Devil straddled the dog, slammed all three of its slavering heads together, and forced them down towards the excrement. The dog was not going to have its nose rubbed in its shit without a fight. First it spread its huge paws wide, then arched its back, and the sweat stood out on the Devil's brow as he struggled to force the animal's snarling heads down. Amazingly enough, the dog appeared to be losing.

Suddenly a voice said, in a very stilted Greek accent, "Fuck off, innit."

The Devil let go of the dog as though it was electrified, and turned to Jesus. "Have I gone totally crazy?" he demanded, "or did that animal just speak?"

It was Cerberus who answered him. "I said 'Fuck off, innit.'"

"Well." The Devil was pacing up and down in agitation. "Let's get today's events in some kind of perspective. First I made a fool of myself trying to tempt you with my bottom. Then I get fined £60 because this creature here can't control its arsehole. And finally, I discover that for the last two and a half thousand years, I have owned a dog that not merely has three heads, but also talks."

"That's life, innit," said the dog.

"Shut it. I was talking to Jesus."

"Well," said Jesus. "It does seem pretty odd that the animal's never spoken to you before."

"Nothing in common, innit?" said the dog. "Stud movies don't interest me, and bones and biting people don't interest him."

"Ooh, I don't know…" said the Devil. "I could just nibble some of those Playgirl centrefolds."

"So," said Jesus to the dog, "do you do any other tricks?"

"Oh, yes! I'll show you."

And with that Cerberus rose onto his hind legs, which made him a full six feet tall, seized the scruff of Jesus's and the Devil's necks in each of his hairy paws, and forced their faces down into the pile of soft, stinking, red hot shit.

Jesus came up gagging and cursing, but the Devil retained enough decorum to quip, "Best thing I've eaten all morning."

"Funny, innit," said the dog, and laughed until he collapsed.

Chapter Five
Sorry, Can't Think Of A Witty Title
For This One.

Billy Bottomley shut the typescript with a snap, and threw it down onto the floor. So much for giving it a second chance: *The Second Coming* was unmitigated crap. Picking up another manuscript at random, he started to read.

Chapter Six
Jack (Again).

It was the kind of night that chilled the stoutest of hearts and set already weakened nerves on edge.

A low, greenish mist clung to the Thames, rising stealthily to envelop the City in a sinister phosphorescent glow. Shop girls hurried home to their lodgings, hearts pounding, and bolted and shuttered their doors behind them, lest their stiff corpses be found in the morning, their features set into a ghastly death rictus. Once inside, they would very quickly pray that their souls might reach the dawn alive.

For throughout the autumn of 1888, a pall of fear had gripped Whitechapel, like the impenetrable murk that now seized its gloomy, cobbled streets. Terrible rumours abounded of a maniac, a disfigured, murderous maniac who savagely slaughtered innocent young girls and left their mutilated bodies as grisly trophies for the sickened Peelers to find.

Yet one figure cut purposefully through the mist, and showed no signs of fear. It was a tall, gaunt man clad elegantly in a swirling black opera cape, which surmounted a hand-tailored dark suit of the finest quality. His thin, mean lips, offset by a pencil-thin moustache, framed a grim and humourless smile. In one of his piercing, coal-black eyes, a monocle glinted; a glossy top hat sat in uneasy repose atop his head.

As he took each measured, near-silent step, he encountered no other human life; until suddenly, a street urchin, dressed in grimy rags, stepped inadvertently into his path. The boy was transfixed in terror, petrified by the gleaming monocle, and caught in the man's evil, whistling breath. Then the sinister figure cried "Begone, boy!", and the lad scuttled back into the mist, offering silent thanks to Jesu that he had escaped with his throat uncut.

The sinister walker resumed his precise, purposeful steps. Out of the mist clattered a hansom cab, its driver braced against the cold and damp. The man flagged down the cab, barked an instruction to the driver, and flopped into the padded upholstery as though exhausted. The driver glanced surreptitiously at the reflection of his eerie client in the mirror, and shuddered involuntarily. Then he whipped the horses, and the hansom hurtled off into the night, and was swallowed up by the fog.

That night, in old London town, there were no fewer than nought savage murders, leaving us to commence our tale on a sunny Tuesday morning in Hemel Hempstead in April 1972.

Chapter Seven
Full Circle.

Bottomley sat back with a pleased smile. Now this was more like it. The book had style, atmosphere and charm. Victorian murder mysteries were perennially popular, and this one was better written than most.

The title – *Warp* – seemed somewhat inappropriate, but he could always contact the author, a certain Richard Falk, and persuade him to substitute an alternative.

Yes! thought Bottomley, this one could be a bestseller, and that was even before the film rights were sold to the highest bidder. It could be just the thing to revive the fortunes of Mackenzie & Dover, not to mention making its author a very wealthy and celebrated man in the process.

Excited, he returned to the manuscript, but stopped reading after just a few pages. For instead of being the magical melodrama he expected, the book instead turned into a very silly tale about an amateur detective chasing a transvestite alien! Rubbish, total rubbish!

Billy Bottomley tossed the book over his shoulder in disgust, and drank his tea.

The End (well, the first of several).

Epilogue.

(Just in case I'm still a bit short on the word count, and to make sure I can charge as much as possible for this book, which this dozen-or-so pages of total nonsense should help to ensure, as indeed should this painfully overlong and totally superfluous subheading.)

La la la la la la la la la la la la la la la la la la la la la
la la la la la la la la la la la la la la la la la la la la la
la la la la la la la la la la la la la la la la la la la la la
la la la la la la la la la la la la la la la la la la la la la
la la la la la la la la la la la la la la la la la la la la la
la la la la la la la la la la la la la la la la la la la la la
la la la la la la la la la la la la la la la la la la la la la
la la la la la la la la la la la la la la la la la la la la la
la la la la la la la la la la la la la la la la la la la la la
la la la la la la la la la la la la la la la la la la la la la
la la la la la la la la la la la la la la la la la la la la la
la la la la la la la la la la la la la la la la la la la la la
la la la la la la la la la la la la la la la la la la la la la
la la la la la la la la la la la la la la la la la la la la la
la la la la la la la la la la la la la la la la la la la la la
la la la la la la la la la la la la la la la la la la la la la
la la la la la la la la la la la la la la la la la la la la la
la la la la la la la la la la la la la la la la la la la la la

la la la la la la la la la la la la la la la la la la la la la
la la la la la la la la la la la la la la la la la la la la la
la la la la la la la la la la la la la la la la la la la la la
la la la la la la la la la la la la la la la la la la la la la
la la la la la la la la la la la la la la la la la la la la la
la la la la la la la la la la la la la la la la la la la la la
la la la la la la la la la la la la la la la bollocks la
la la la la la la la la la la la la la la la la la la la la la
la la la la la la la la la la la la la la la la la la la la la
la la la la la la la la la la la la la la la la la la la la la
la la la la la la la la la la la la la la la la la la la la la
la la la la la la la la la la la la la la la la la la la la la
la la la la la la la la la la la la la la la la la la la la la
la la la la la la la la la la la la la la la la la la la la la
la la la la la la la la la la la la la la la la la la la la la
la la la la la la la la la la la la la la la la la la la la la
la la la la la la la la la la la la la la la la la la la la la
la la la la la la la la la la la la la la la la la la la la la
la la la la la la la la la la la la la la la la la la la la la
la la la la la la la la la la la la la la la la la la la la la
la la la la la la la la la la la la la la la la la la la la la
la la la la la la la la la la la la la la la la la la la la la
la la la la la la la la la la la la la la la la la la la la la
la la la la la la la la la la la la la la la la la la la la la
la la la la la la la la la la la la la la la la la la la la la
la la la la la la la la la la la la la la la la la la la la la
la la la la la la la la la la la la la la la la la la la la la
la la la la la la la la la la la la la la la la la la la la la
la la la la la la la la la la la la la la la la la la la la la
la la la la la la la la la la la la la la la la la la la la la
la la la la la la la la la la la la la la la la la la la la la
la la la la la la la la la la la la la la la la la la la la la

la la la la la la la la la la la la la la la la la la la la la la
la la la la la la la la la la la la la la la la la la la la la la
la la la la la la la la la la la la la la la la la la la la la la
la la la la la la la la la la la la la la la la la la la la la la
la la la la la la la la la la la la la la la la la la la la la la
la la la la la la la la la la la la la la la la la la la la la la
la la la la la la la la la la la la la la la la la la la la la la
la la la la la la la la la la la la la la la la la la la la la la
la la la la la la la la la la la la la la la la la la la la la la
la la la la la la la la la la la la la la la la la la la la la la
la la la la la la la la la la la la la la la la la la la la la la
la la la la la la la la la la la la la la la la la la la la la la
la la la la la la la la la la la la la la la la la la la la la la
la la la la la la la la la la la la la la la la la la la la la la
la la la la la la la la la la la la la la la la la la la la la la
la la la la la la la la la la la la la la la la la la la la la la
elephant's fanny la la la la la la la la la la la la la la la
la la la la la la la la la la la la la la la la la la la la la la
la la la la la la la la la la la la la la la la la la la la la la
la la la la la la la la la la la la la la la la la la la la la la
la la la la la la la la la la la la la la la la la la la la la la
la la la la la la la la la la la la la la la la la la la la la la
la la la la la la la la la la la la la la la la la la la la la la
la la la la la la la la la la la la la la la la la la la la la la
la la la la la la la la la la la la la la la la la la la la la la
la la la la la la la la la la la la la la la la la la la la la la
la la la la la la la la la la la la la la la la la la la la la la
la la la la la la la la la la la la la la la la la la la la la la
la la la la la la la la la la la la la la la la la la la la la la
la la la la la la la la la la la la la la la la la la la la la la
la la la la la la la la la la la la la la la la la la la la la la
la la la la la la la la la la la la la la la la la la la la la la

la la la la la la la la la la la la la la la la la la la la la la la
la la la la la la la la la la la la la la la la la la la la la la la
la la la la la la la la la la la la la la la la la la la la la la la
la la la la la la la la la la la la la la la la la la la la la la la
la la la la la la la la la la la la la la la la la la la la la la la
la la la la la la la la la la la la la la la la la la la la la la la
la la la la la la la la la la la la la la la la la la la la la la la
la la la la la la la la la la la la la la la la la la la la la la la
la la la la la la la la la la la la la la la la la la la la la la la
la la la la la la la la la la la la la la la la la la la la la la la
la la la la la la la la la la la la la la la la la la la la la la la
la la la la la la la la la la la la la la la la la la la la la la la
la la la la la la la la la la la la la la la la la la la la la la la
la la la la la la la la la la la la la la la la la la la la la la la
la la la la la la la la la la la la la la la la la la la la la la la
la la la la la la la la la la la la la la la la la la la la la la la
la la la la la la la la la la la la la la la la la la la la la la la
la la la la la la la la la la la la la la la la la la la la la la la
la la la la la la la la la la la la la la la la la la la la la la la
la la la la la la la la la la la la la la la la la la la la la la la
la la la la la la la la la la la la la la la la la la la la la la la
la la la la la la la la la la la la la la la la la la la la la la la
la la la la la la la la la la la la la la la la la la la la la la la
la la la la la la la la la la la la la la la la la la la la la la la
underage sex la la la la la la la la la la la la la la la la la la la
la la la la la la la la la la la la la la la la la la la la la la la
la la la la la la la la la la la la la la la la la la la la la la la
la la la la la la la la la la la la la la la la la la la la la la la
la la la la la la la la la la la la la la la la la la la la la la la
la la la la la la la la la la la la la la la la la la la la la la la
la la la la la la la la la la la la la la la la la la la la la la la
la la la la la la la la la la la la la la la la la la la la la la la

la la la la la la la la la la la la la la la la la la la la la la
la la la la la la la la la la la la la la la la la la la la la la
la la la la la la la la la la la la la la la la la la la la la la
la la la la la la la la la la la la la la la la la la la la la la
la la la la la la la la la la la la la la la la la la la la la la
la la la la la la la la la la la la la la la la la la la la la la
la la la la la la la la la la la la la la la la la la la la la la
la la la la la la la la la la la la la la la la la la la la la la
la la la la la la la la la la la la la la la la la la la la la la
la la la la la la la la la la la la la la la la la la la la la la
la la la la la la la la la la la la la la la la la la la la la la
la la la la la la la la la la la la la la la la la la la la la la
la la la la la la la la la la la la la la la la la la la la la la
la la la la la la la la la la la la la la la la la la la la la la
la la la la la la la la la la la la la la la la la la la la la la
la la la la la la la la la la la la la la la la la la la la la la
la la la la la la la la la la la la la la la la la la la la la la
la la la la la la la la la la la la la la la la la la la la la la
la la la la la la la la la la la la la la la la la la la la la la
la la la la la la la la la la la la la la la la la la la la la la
la la la la la la la la la la la la la la la la la la la la la la
la la la la la la la la la la la la la la la la la la la la la la
la la la la la la la la la la la la la la la la la la la la la la
la la la la la la la la la la la la la la la la la la la la la la
la la la la la la la la la la la la la la la la la la la la la la
la la la la la la la la la la la la la la la la la la la la la la
la la la la la la la la la la la la la la la la la la la la la la
la la la la la la la la la la la la la la la la la la la la la la
la la la la la la la la la la la la la la la la la la la la la la
la la la la la la la la la la la la la la la la la la la la la la
la la la la la la la la la la la la la la la la la la la la la la
la la la la la la la la la la la la la la la la la la la la la la
la la la la la la la la la la la la la la la la la la la la la la

la la la la la la la la la la la la la la la la la la la la la la la
la la la la la la la la la la la la la la la la la la la la la la la
la la la la la la la la la la la la la la la la la la la la la la la
la la la la la la la la la la la la la la la la la la la la la la la
la la la la la la la la la la la la la la la la la la la la la la la
la la la la la la la la la la la la la la la la la la la la la la la
la la la la la la la la la la la la la la la la la la la la la la la
la la la la la la la la la la la la la la la la la la la la la la la
la la la la la la la la la la la la la la la la la la la la la la la
la la la la la la la la la la la la la la la la la la la la la la la
la la la la la la la la la la la la la la la la la la la la la la la
la la la la la la la la la la la la la la la la la la la la la la la
la la la la la la la la la la la la la la la la la la la la la la la
la la la la la la la la la la la la la la la la la la la la la la la
la la la la la la la la la la la la la la la la blowjob la la la la
la la la la la la la la la la la la la la la la la la la la la la la
la la la la la la la la la la la la la la la la la la la la la la la
la la la la la la la la la la la la la la la la la la la la la la la
la la la la la la la la la la la la la la la la la la la la la la la
la la la la la la la la la la la la la la la la la la la la la la la
la la la la la la la la la la la la la la la la la la la la la la la
la la la la la la la la la la la la la la la la la la la la la la la
la la la la la la la la la la la la la la la la la la la la la la la
la la la la la la la la la la la la la la la la la la la la la la la
la la la la la la la la la la la la la la la la la la la la la la la
la la la la la la la la la la la la la la la la la la la la la la la
la la la la la la la la la la la la la la la la la la la la la la la
la la la la la la la la la la la la la la la la la la la la la la la
la la la la la la la la la la la la la la la la la la la la la la la
la la la la la la la la la la la la la la la la la la la la la la la
la la la la la la la la la la la la la la la la la la la la la la la
la la la la la la la la la la la la la la la la la la la la la la la
la la la la la la la la la la la la la la la la la la la la la la la

la la la la la la la la la la la la la la la la la la la la la la
la la la la la la la la la la la la la la la la la la la la la la
la la la la la la la la la la la la la la la la la la la la la la
la la la la la la la la la la la la la la la la la la la la la la
la la la la la la la la la la la la la la la la la la la la la la
la la la la la la la la la la la la la la la la la la la la la la
la la la la la la la la la la la la la la la la la la la la la la
la la la la la la la la la la la la la la la la la la la la la la
la la la la la la la la la la la la la la la la la la la la la la
la la la la la la la la la la la la la la la la la la la la la la
la la la la la la la la la la la la la la la la la la la la la la
la la la la la la la la la la la la la la la la la la la la la la
la la la la la la la la la la la la la la la la la la la la la la
la la la la la la la la la la la la la la la la la la la la la la
la la la la la la la la la la la la la la la la la la la la la la
la la la la la la la la la la la la la la la la la la la la la la
la la la la la la la la la la la la la la la la la la la la la la
la la la la la la la la la la la la la la la la la la la la la la
la la la la la la la la la la la la la la la la la la la la la la
la la la la la la la la la la la la la la la la la la la la la la
la la la la la la la la la la la la la la la la la la la la la la
la la la la la la la la la la la la la la la la la la la la la la
la la la la la la la la la la la la la la la la la la la la la la
la la la la la la la la la la la la la la la la la la la la la la
la la la la la la la la la la la la la la la la la la la la la la
la la la la la la la la la la la la la la la la la la la la la la
la la la la la la la la la la la la la la la la la la la la la la
la la la la la la la la la la la la la la la la la la naked
schoolgirl la la la la la la la la la la la la la la la la
la la la la la la la la la la la la la la la la la la la la la la
la la la la la la la la la la la la la la la la la la la la la la

la la la la la la la la la la la la la la la la la la la la la la
la la la la la la la la la la la la la la la la la la la la la la
la la la la la la la la la la la la la la la la la la la la la la
la la la la la la la la la la la la la la la la la la la la la la
la la la la la la la la la la la la la la la la la la la la la la
la la la la la la la la la la la la la la la la la la la la la la
la la la la la la la la la la la la la la la la la la la la la la
la la la la la la la la la la la la la la la la la la la la la la
la la la la la la la la la la la la la la la la la la la la la la
la la la la la la la la la la la la la la la la la la la la la la
la la la la la la la la la la la la la la la la la la la la la la
la la la la la la la la la la la la la la la la la la la la la la
la la la la la la la la la la la la la la la la la la la la la la
la la la la la la la la la la la la la la la la la la la la la la
la la la la la la la la la la la la la la la la la la la la la la
la la la la la la la la la la la la la la la la la la la la la la
la la la la la la la la la la la la la la la la la la la la la la
la la la la la la la la la la la la la la la la la la la la la la
la la la la la la la la la la la la la la la la la la la la la la
la la la la la la la la la la la la la la la la la la la la la la
la la la la la la la la la la la la la la la la la la la la la la
la la la la la la la la la la la la la la la la la la la la la la
la la la la la la la la la la la la la la la la la la la la la la
la la la la la la la la la la la la la la la la la la la la la la
la la la la la la la la la la la la la la la la la la la la la la
la la la la la la la la la la la la la la la la la la la la la la
la la la la la la la la la la la la la la la la la la la la la la
la la la la la la la la la la la la la la la la la la la la la la
la la la la la la la la la la la la la la la la la la la la la la
la la la la la la la la la la la la la la la la la la la la la la
la la la la la la la la la la la la la la la la la la la la la la
la la la la la la la la la la la la la la la la la la la la la la
la la la la la la la la la la la la la la la la la la la la la la
la la la la la la la la la la la la la la la la la la la la la la

la la la la la la la la la la la la la la la la la la la la la la la
la la la la la la la la la la la la la la la la la la la la la la la
la la la la la la la la la la la la la la la la la la la la la la la
la la la la la la la la la la la la la la la la la la la la la la la
la la la la la la la la la la la la la la la la la la la la la la la
la la la la la la la la la la la la la la la la la la la la la la la
la la la la la la la la la la la la la la la la la la la la la la la
la la la la la la la la la la la la la la la la la la la la la la la
la la la la la la la la la la la la la la la la la la la la la la la
la la la la la la la la la la la la la la la la la la la la la la la
la la la la la la la la la la la la la la la la la la la la la la la
la la la la la la la la la la la la la la la la la la la la la la la
la la la la la la la la la la la la la la la la la la la la la la la
la la la la la la la la la la la la la la la la la la la la la la la
la la la la la la la la la la la la la la la la la la la la la la la
la la la la la la la la la la la la la la la la la la la la la la la
la la la la la la la la la la la la la la la la la la la la la la la
la la la la la la la la la la la la la la la la la la la la la la la
la la la la la la la la la la la la la la la la la la la la la la la
la la la la la la la la la la la la la la la la la la la la la la la
la la la la la la la la la la la la la la la la la la la la la la la
la la la la la la la la la another smutty subliminal
message la la la la la la la la la la la la la la la la la la
la la la la la la la la la la la la la la la la la la la la la la la
la la la la la la la la la la la la la la la la la la la la la la la
la la la la la la la la la la la la la la la la la la la la la la la
la la la la la la la la la la la la la la la la la la la la la la la
la la la la la la la la la la la la la la la la la la la la la la la
la la la la la la la la la la la la la la la la la la la la la la la
la la la la la la la la la la la la la la la la la la la la la la la
la la la la la la la la la la la la la la la la la la la la la la la
la la la la la la la la la la la la la la la la la la la la la la la

la la la la la la la la la la la la la la la la la la la la la la
la la la la la la la la la la la la la la la la la la la la la la
la la la la la la la la la la la la la la la la la la la la la la
la la la la la la la la la la la la la la la la la la la la la la
la la la la la la la la la la la la la la la la la la la la la la
la la la la la la la la la la la la la la la la la la la la la la
la la la la la la la la la la la la la la la la la la la la la la
la la la la la la la la la la la la la la la la la la la la la la
la la la la la la la la la la la la la la la la la la la la la la
la la la la la la la la la la la la la la la la la la la la la la
la la la la la la la la la la la la la la la la la la la la la la
la la la la la la la la la la la la la la la la la la la la la la
la la la la la la la la la la la la la la la la la la la la la la
la la la la la la la la la la la la la la la la la la la la la la
la la la la la la la la la la la la la la la la la la la la la la
la la la la la la la la la la la la la la la la la la la la la la
la la la la la la la la la la la la la la la la la la la la la la
la la la la la la la la la la la la la la la la la la la la la la
la la la la la la la la la la la la la la la la la la la la la la
la la la la la la la la la la la la la la la la la la la la la la
la la la la la la la la la la la la la la la la la la la la la la
la la la la la la la la la la la la la la la la la la la la la la
la la la la la la la la la la la la la la la la la la la la la la
la la la la la la la la la la la la la la la la la la la la la la
la la la la la la la la la la la la la la la la la la la la la la
la la la la la la la la la la la la la la la la la la la la la la
la la la la la la la la la la la la la la la la la la la la la la
la la la la la la la la la la la la la la la la la la la la la la
la la la la la la la la la la la la la la la la la la la la la la
la la la la la la la la la enormous breasts la la la la la
la la la la la la la la la la la la la la la la la la la la la la

la la la la la la la la la la la la la la la la la la la la la
la la la la la la la la la la la la la la la la la la la la la
la la la la la la la la la la la la la la la la la la la la la
la la la la la la la la la la la la la la la la la la la la la
la la la la la la la la la la la la la la la la la la la la la
la la la la la la la la la la la la la la la la la la la la la
la la la la la la la la la la la la la la la la la la la la la
la la la la la la la la la la la la la la la la la la la la la
la la la la la la la la la la la la la la la la la la la la la
la la la la la la la la la la la la la la la la la la la la la
la la la la la la la la la la la la la la la la la la la la la
la la la la la la la la la la la la la la la la la la la la la
la la la la la la la la la la la la la la la la la la la la la
la la la la la la la la la la la la la la la la la la la la la
la la la la la la la la la la la la la la la la la la la la la
la la la la la la la la la la la la la la la la la la la la la
la la... thank God for cut-and-paste commands
on the modern word processor, or typing all
these la-las would be like a Mavis Beacon typing
exercise... anyway, just about there, you'll be
pleased to know... just a few more for luck... la
la la la la la la la la la la la la la la la la la la la la
la la la la la la la la la la la la la la la la la la la la
la la la la la la la la la la la la la la la la la la la la
la la la la la la la la la la la la la la la la la la... OWW,
FUCKING HELL! WHAT WAS THAT?

God: *That was me, punching you in the head. I want a word with you about that blasphemous section earlier.*

Jesus: *And so do I.*

Author: *Oww... fuck... don't you start as well.*

God: *Well? What have you got to say for yourself?*

Author: *I didn't write it, you see... well, not really. It was a book within a book. I had the Bottomley character say how tasteless and offensive it was.*

God: *A flimsy defence. Not only was it blasphemous, it was also completely and utterly inaccurate. I never made a bird called Michelle in Basildon pregnant.*

Author: *Well, in that case, I apologise unreservedly.*

God: *Her name was Tracy and she came from Romford... shit! SHIT!*

Jesus: *Let the cat out of the bag there, eh, Dad?*

God: *Shut it, you little fucker.*

Jesus: *And I've got a complaint, too... portraying me as a lager lout who eats vindaloos just to impress his mates.*

Author: *Yes, of course. I know that really you're the source of purity, and you drink only nectar and eat gossamer-like manna…*

Jesus: *Are ye calling me a puff, like?*

(No, I don't know why he's suddenly acquired an unconvincing Geordie accent either.)

Manna is fur homs, man! In my drinkin' club, yer a fuckin' black-balled puff if yer eat anythin' less than a phall. I eat phalls, man!

(The spellchecker on my word processor actually changed this last statement to "I eat phallus,man!" I'd better not,though–this book is quite blasphemous enough already…)

Vindaloos is for puffs! Gan on Dad, let's knack 'im!

God: *Aye! An' he spilt my pint!*

Jesus: *Gan on, lamp the fucker!*

Author: *Yee-owch.*

God: *Lee-amp.*

Author: *Yee-owch.*

Jesus: *Lee-amp.*

Author: *Yee-owch.*

God: *Lee-amp.*

Author: *Yee-owch.*

Jesus: *Lee-amp.*

Author: *Yee-owch.*

God: *Lee-amp.*

Author: *Yee-owch.*

Jesus: *Lee-amp.*

Author: *Yee-owch.*

God: *Lee-amp.*

Author: *Yee-owch.*

Jesus: *Lee-amp.*

Author: *Yee-owch.*

God: *Lee-amp.*

Author: *Yee-owch.*

Jesus: *Lee-amp.*

Author: *Yee-owch.*

Reader: *Stop it, all of you! This is just another ploy to waste space, and make the book look better value on the shelf. This is getting as boring as the la-las, so put a sock in it.*

God: *Shit. Miserable bastard.*

Jesus: *Yes, I was just enjoying myself.*

Author: *Well, I wasn't.*

God: *Shut it. Lee-amp – right in the knackers!*

Author: *Ooh, me fuckin' gonads.*

Devil: *Did someone mention male genitalia?*

God: *What do you want, you great woofter?*

Devil: *Can I join in? Please?*

Jesus: *Be my guest.*

Reader: *Look, this book's been quite obscene enough already. Let's have a nice scene with some friendly bunnies gambolling in the grass, some nice children playing with their…*

Devil: *Ooh, you're a big boy.*

God: *Gan on Satan, fuck 'im!*

Jesus: *Fuck 'im!*

Author: *Fuck 'im!*

Devil: *I fully intend to.*

Reader: *Yee-owwl, my jacksie! Me fuckin' ring's on fire! I'm going to wake up with a ringpiece like a doughnut, etc.*

The End (or is it?)

Hidden Bonus Chapter.

(Well, if rock stars can try this trick to make their poxy CDs look longer, why can't I?)

Bob Shandie sat back in his plush red chair at the Dorchester Hotel, and sipped his champagne. How strangely things had turned out for children's television during 1973, how strangely…

"Ladies and gentlemen," said the MC. "Welcome to the fifteenth annual Children's TV Awards. I trust you've all enjoyed your dinners…" Murmurs of assent. "Now, without further ado, let me present the first of tonight's awards… for 'Best New TV Concept For The Under-Fives'. And the shortlisted programmes are… *The Animals Of Hampton Dell, Juggy And His Friend* and *Geoff The Gynaecologist.* And before I announce the winner, industry experts will note that this is the first time since 1969 that Hande-Shandie International haven't dominated this category. Rumour has it, scripts for all three shows were presented to them, but rejected… and instead all three were produced by the new kid on the block, and now their main competitor, Off-The-Wrist Productions Ltd. And the winner is…" he opened the envelope. "*Geoff The Gynaecologist.*"

There was a roar of applause, and a beaming

Maurice Selkirk made for the stage. Les Hande and Bob Shandie glanced ruefully at one another, laughed, and swigged more champagne. Setbacks like this were inevitable in business, and Hande-Shandie International would be back in force for the 1974 awards. After all, the firm's new series, created especially to exploit the burgeoning 'adult-infant TV market', was premiering on February 19th 1974, and was bound to be a big hit.

Yes, reflected Bob Shandie, draining the last of his champagne, *Peter The Shit-Eating Necrophiliac Serial Paedophile* was bound to go down in history as one of the kids' TV greats. It might even eclipse *Skydog And Webcat* and *Ali Butt And His Fishy Friends*. Not to mention Billy The Bedouin And His Ay-rabs.

The End (Yes. Really!)

Appendices.

Appendix One.

Election Results for the constituency of Shoreham & Otford
Thursday 18th June 1970

Sir JSP Shertliffe-Tor	Conservative	24,386	56.3%
Dr IAMA Fencesitter	Liberal	12,711	29.3%
Fred *"middle names is for soft Southern jessies"* Plebbyobb	Labour	6,016	13.9%
RA Cyst	National Front	186	0.4%
Herr Adolf Streicher-Goering	Oswald Moseley Appreciation	39	0.1%
Peter *"Fnarr Fnarr Mrs."* Smith	Unfunny Raving Pillock	6	0.0%
Angus MacTavish	Independent Scottish Nationalist	3	0.0%
	Majority	11,675	**26.9%**

Electorate: 60,881. Turnout: 71.2%. Conservative hold.

Appendix Two.

Complete lyrics to *Fatty Fatima*
by Billy The Bedouin And His Ay-rabs

I met her way out in the desert
Where the sun was shinin' bright
She's a girl I'd never desert
'Cos she's my shinin' light

Her love makes me richer
Than any very rich sheikh
And if that girl should leave
It'd make my poor heart break

Wo-oh fatty fatty Fatima
For me she's the one
'Cos she's got a tum like a camel-skin drum
And she makes my heart go b-boom
Yeah, she makes my heart go b-boom!

She's got more flesh
Than the fleshpots of Cairo
Think I'll write a love poem
With my Biro

'Bout her almond eyes
And her bright red lips
And the couple of spare tyres
Around her hips

Wo-oh fatty fatty Fatima
For me she's the one
'Cos she's got a tum like a camel-skin drum
And she makes my heart go b-boom
Yeah, she makes my heart go b-boom!

Gonna make her an Eastern promise
I'll stay by her side
I wouldn't swap my Fatima
For a thousand camel rides

When she fell into my arms
I said "Gotcha!"
And I love the fact
She ain't no weight-watcher

Wo-oh fatty fatty Fatima
For me she's the one
'Cos she's got a tum like a camel-skin drum
And she makes my heart go b-boom
Yeah, she makes my heart go b-boom!

[Repeat chorus about 17,000 times]

Music and lyrics © Browne/Starr.
Published by Chocolate Starfish Music/Clamjoust Songs, 1965.

Appendix Three.

**Detective Inspector (formerly Sergeant) Harry
Hogg's citation for the George Medal for
Conspicuous Bravery, 12th January 1976**

Her Majesty is pleased to present to
DETECTIVE INSPECTOR HAROLD HORATIO
HENRY HOGG the GEORGE MEDAL FOR
CONSPICUOUS GALLANTRY on this twelfth
day of January in the year of our Lord nineteen
hundred and seventy six.

Whereupon we celebrate that upon the
seventeenth day of September nineteen hundred
and seventy five the said Harold Hogg did, with
total disregared for his own safety, surprise and
arrest dangerous armed hostage takers at the
Hemel Hempstead factory of Billy Butler &
Company (Biscuits) Ltd. by eating through a six
foot barricade of chocolate nobhobs, citron cakes,
garibaldis and world-famous frangipane cookies,
prices for which start from as little as 12p.

In recognition of his bravery, the said Billy Butler
& Company (Biscuits) Ltd. offered Detective
Inspector Hogg as many free biscuits as he
could eat in a week, and consequently went
into bankruptcy shortly before Christmas. It is
understood that the present Labour Government
is to nationalise the firm and relaunch it as
British Biscuits.

– Elizabeth R.

Appendix Four.

Extracts from the original estate agents' particulars for Hell *(as bought by the Devil)*:

Messrs. Oxtaby, Dennison & Mallahide
Purveyors of Fine and Unusual Homes

"Hades"

This charming and tasteful property offers exceptionally spacious accommodation for Supreme Beings of Evil, and comes complete with all facilities for the eternal torment of up to 63,000,000,000,000 souls. Extensively refurbished and modernised by the current owner, its many unusual facilities include:

En-Suite Three Headed Dog

Included at no extra cost, this charming and playful fellow is fully house-trained, and makes both a loving pet and a loyal guard dog. Particularly fond of children, although he should not be given them between meals.

The property also offers fishing rights in the River Styx, so is especially well suited to Supreme Beings of Evil who are keen anglers.

Price: £380,000,000,000.

Viewing strictly by appointment.
Please contact Mr. Brendon Pierce
of our Park Lane office for further details.

Appendix Five.

Dinner menu at the Roupettes-Sur-La-Langue
Restaurant, Le Château De Porc-Sourde,
Rideaux-De-Boeuf, 27th July 1969
(the day David-François-Pierre-Paul Je-Me-Suis-Reveillé-Ce-Matin tried acid for the first and only time).

Le Diner

Amuse-Gueule
Tranche de Yaourt à Boire, Garni de Jambon
Poisson de Mer (Encore dans la Mer)
Sorbet au Aéroglisseur
Pavé de Boeuf Surréalist, Sauce Chemin de Fer
Les Fromages de Loup,
Cochon et Chat Hongrois
Confiture Rôti avec Jus de Pommes de Terre
Un Homme avec une Cafetière sur sa Cafetière

60F – SERVICE COMPRIS

English translation (for those who need it):

Dinner Menu

Chef's Complimentary Starter
Slice of Drinking Yoghurt,
Garnished with Ham
Sea Fish (Still in the Sea)
Hovercraft Sorbet
Fillet Steak "Surrealist" with Railway Sauce
Wolf, Pig and Hungarian Cat Cheeses
Roast Jam with Potato Sauce
A Man with a Coffee Pot on his Head

60 FRANCS INCLUDING SERVICE

Blank pages like this kill trees and waste paper
(except of course this page isn't,
technically speaking, blank).